AF480666

THE CALL

*For those who answered the call
and went a different way.*

Micah Lee Malloy

"What you have known as health is a state of dormancy.
Health and vitality is when you feel the invigoration
and stimulation of new life beginning.
You have not experienced health yet.
Not until you have switched on all the
cosmic elements of your body."

Rebecca Dawson channeling the Masters,
How to Thrive as a New Human, 2023

DEDICATION

I would like to thank:

The indomitable Anne Parks, who founded The Center for Human Unfolding in her living room in Santa Barbara in 1980. Then she formed The School of Intuitive Massage. I had the great fortune of attending and then becoming an intuitive massage instructor. When I told Anne I had enrolled in Acupuncture school, she said, "you becoming an acupuncturist is like a gypsy trying to learn how to do ballet."

Elliot Cowen for his beautiful Plant Spirit Medicine class. We spent a year, all four seasons, being introduced to five elements acupuncture, how to journey as a shaman and how to work with the plants as a plant spirit medicine practitioner.

Dr Pang and Wisdom Healing Zhineng Qi Gong, the Medicineless Hospital and the collective shift he provided for humanity.

A special thank you to Rebecca Dawson, whose channeled wisdom inspired much of this work and whose encouragement helped me bring this book into form.

TABLE OF CONTENTS:

Dedication vii

Preface.. 3

The Call 5

Taste.. 6

She Said 7

Now Versus Then 9

Energy Bronco 10

Magic goes That-A-Ways 11

Is the Body a Translator for Multidimensional Consciousness.... 12

You are Filling up with Gold 13

How Do you Catch a Ghost.................................... 14

The Rules of Reality 15

The Secret that Would Have Killed Me 16

The Currency of Inspiration 17

The Weight of my Life... 19

Awakening into Form.. 20

Your Body Belongs to the Earth 21

Refreshment 22

I Am Being Taken over by Gentleness 23

Armor Piercing Puffballs 25

Enjoy the Miracle of Who You Are......................... 26

Innate is Making Art 27

When the Body Takes Over..................................... 28

Earth Element is Codes for Creation 29

Posture and Imposter... 30

Putting on My Skin Suit... 31

TABLE OF CONTENTS:

The Sharpness of the Kaleidoscope 33

Truths That You Feel 34

It's a Reverberation Day.. 35

The Familiarity of the Unknown 36

Let Yourself Disappear... 37

We Keep Behaving 38

Squatting in the Center of the Galaxy 39

Step Into your Light Suit.. 41

The Adolescent Shelf 42

Chuck Your Pride 43

Self Driving Body 44

Your Biology is Tethered to a Certain Timeline......................... 45

You Are All That Matters 46

The New Flavor of Sovereignty 47

The Body Goes Round and Round.. 49

Papers Boats 50

Without An Identity 51

Be Still 52

From Dizzy Spells to Presence Spells 53

My Personality is a Passenger 54

I Just Had the Dizzy Spell of Dizzy Spells................................. 55

Today I Got so Close to my Broken Heart 56

Most of the Feeling in My Body is an Echo 57

Earth Gravity Versus Cosmic Gravity 59

Being Undefended... 60

Self Worth.. 61

TABLE OF CONTENTS:

To Love the Pain 62

The Pool 63

The Sound of Gold 64

Some of the Building Blocks of Me are Made of Pain 65

Crossing the Threshold 67

Get Out of the Box 68

This Movement, This Expression 69

I'm Someone Who Answers 70

The Nature of Nature 71

Possibility 72

Ride The Pain 73

Paint Me with Lines of Gold 75

Everything You Know About Your Body 76

Sleepwalking Towards Destiny 77

Pressure 78

If You Become Involved in the Narrative 79

Shamanic Journey 80

I Don't Feel like Saying Anything Meaningful 81

Love Debris 83

There Is No Consequence 84

Is Potential a Substance 85

Within Your Waters 86

Talk to the Creator 87

Feelings Travel at the Speed of Light 88

Codependence 89

I Am the Seam 91

TABLE OF CONTENTS:

I Know What the Singularity Is 93

Glimpsing Immorality 95

Connection 96

Longing Connects You with Connection 97

Drop Through the Chessboard and Free Your DNA 99

The Longing Channel 100

There is Nowhere That I am Not 101

Micah's Dream Last Night 102

Self Driving Body 2 – Effortlessness 104

Doing and Being Are One 105

Coyote Medicine 107

Who Is Driving 108

Ordinary Sacred Space 109

I Am Bones 110

Stand Naked 111

Open Blue Sky 112

The Bridge to Nowhere 113

Is Your Mind a Good Servant to You 114

Double Bind 115

Sweet Medicine 117

Destiny 118

Zero Point 119

An Enhanced Reality 120

There's a Dark Residue 121

Self Loathing 123

TABLE OF CONTENTS:

You Are Beginning to Recognize Yourself 124

Words From the Body 125

Embracing the One Who Plods and Plots 127

If You Knew How Much You are Loved 128

Nausea 129

Show Yourself to Yourself 131

The Gift of Self Loathing... 132

I Am Making a Pact With Myself 135

Power Spots Magnify What We Know............................. 136

It Doesn't Matter 137

The Era of Disruption 138

Pain Is Power... 139

Playing Death Like an Accordion 141

Scraping the Bottom of the Beaker 142

The Universe Breathes Through Us................................ 143

High Tide... 145

Here I Am 146

Things That Make Themselves Happen 147

Summon Yourself... 149

Form Appearing 150

Let Your Discomfort Catch up With You 151

The Center of All Things.. 152

The Curde Algo Versus You 153

The Price You Pay... 155

The Waterfall... 156

TABLE OF CONTENTS:

I Am a Common Woman.. 157

Sitting With Star Command 159

Embrace Your Insecurity 160

The Basement of the Basement..................................... 161

My Body Is Taking Over Again 162

Do I Dare Feel This Good.. 163

The Whalers 165

Where Are You?.. 166

I Speak Tree.. 167

Lifecycle of a Grasshopper 169

Dissolving 170

Innocence.. 171

Come Out of the Cave 172

Scruffy Perfection... 173

We Have Returned 175

Meet Micah Lee Malloy, LAc.LMT 177

Image Index 181

PREFACE

This little book is an introduction to the multidimensional body. It is an exploration of the new paradigm of health, healing and eternal life. It is not based on science or the scientific method. It is not the philosophy of a master or a series of concepts that build upon one another and ultimately justify my perspective. It is, instead, journal notes and spontaneous poetry that try to capture, as they are happening, ineffable moments of pure inspired glory. Moments that glimpse the sacred stepping into form. It is a record of raw, unfiltered direct experiences of one person's journey of self-discovery. There is no external authority for what I have shared. Instead, it is a growing understanding that the grasp of the levers of reality lie deep within. We are the creators of reality and in this, we are the creators of our beliefs, our programming, our health and well-being, our immortality or our demise. Within my words I hope to share the spark of self-disclosure and how powerful and essential it is in igniting our awakening. There is nothing of more value than your authentic expression. That is the gold worth mining. In your awakening, the voice you must inevitably hear is your own. The call you must hear is within you and the ultimate authority in all things is the sovereignty of your being.

THE CALL

The meaning of the miracle
Is in the hearing of the Call.

All the walls have fallen.
You stand upon the clearing.
You sit upon your throne.

The Sovereign of your life.

TASTE

The taste of who I really am
Is like swallowing lightning.
Is like a silver winged buzzard
Soaring over my tongue
   and disappearing
     into the orange horizon
at the back of my mouth,
    dissolving into my blood.
I gasp as something thicker than air
    explodes in my lungs
and angels take command of my voice
and trumpet their song out of my throat.

I am sound,
I am sensation,
I am taste,
I am now and
I am not this poem.

SHE SAID

She said into my discouraged eyes, "you're on your way. Where you were is not bad, not less than where you are now. Even though you've always made it so, you can make it different now. You don't have to cross out where you were.

What I've been seeking has been seeking me. Acting from a place of coherence is its own reward.

NOW VERSUS THEN

I am the spots on a leopard.

I am the camouflage on a frog.

I'm the bend in a river.

I'm the hollow in an ancient, fallen log.

I've got a box of trophies

Gathering dust in my garage.

And some siblings in the Midwest

Who stayed the course and did their best

And now they've grown rich

At their jobs.

ENERGY BRONCO

Grab hold of your reality.

Like a cowboy roping a bronking buck.

Bucking bronc.

Only it's energetic.

Energy bronco.

Dyslexia is part of the game,

        the koan,

            the riddle

That unwinds your mind.

Grab hold of your reality.

MAGIC GOES THAT-A-WAYS

Magic goes that-a-ways.
It's a mystery in a language
      you don't speak.
What looked like a narrow road
      is now the sky

The music lifts you up
You lift the music up.
How are you doing this?

IS THE BODY A TRANSLATOR FOR MULTIDIMENSIONAL CONCIOUSNESS?

Is it a way to "grab hold" of 3d reality? Formless into form. I'm feeling the translation of multidimensional consciousness into everyday reality with my body. It's ecstatic and primal at the same time. It feels like the formless, expanded-self part of me extends itself through my head, heart and chest, down my arms and into my hands. It's like I'm putting on a suit of light and taking off a suit of armor. I have the sense that the super subtle part of me is grabbing hold of reality using my body. I'm possessing myself. My back pain just vanished. Inspirational realizations eradicate aches. It keeps happening. The aches come back but I'm incrementally less afraid. I'm getting a whole new body. Inside is white silk.

You are filling up with gold so that you can give it all away and then do it all over again. This is openness without giving yourself away. Openness with discernment. No more unspoken hoping to be accepted. Will you adopt me? Are you my family? Are you my missing piece? Are you my missing peace? The hole inside is gone now. You can accept them all. *No harm will come to you.*

What are you made of? Light? Energy? Not an idea, it's real. Can you feel in your body the building blocks of light? Can you feel the building blocks of belief? You are more than the sum of your beliefs. You are beliefs, plus light, plus organic form, plus emotion. See yourself as very, very big. A cloud of code surrounds you. Light code, color code and you select the codes that create your form. You create yourself as you go, consciously, unconsciously and subconsciously. It all works in a perfect concert. You are a symphony. You are all the players and the conductor and more. You are the instruments of sound and light. Think of it. You are the instrument that you create and then you play yourself throughout your day. Trees do it, birds do it but you have something extra. Your capacity to change your form is unlimited.

HOW DO YOU CATCH A GHOST?

You sneak up on it
        where it's hiding
In the corner
        of your discomfort.

Where shadows
        are more than shadows.
Where the dust
        doesn't rise.

You have to move quieter than air
        till the atoms themselves
        are at your command.

THE RULES OF REALITY

The rules of reality are more important than your needs. So learn the rules of reality to have what you need. This was my subconscious belief formed during infancy. My mother believed in a stingy reality. One that did not easily give up its rewards. I transposed the meaning. Other people's needs take precedence, in a reality creating sort of way. I bow to others' realities. I shut down my own reality creating abilities. I can change my world now that I am aware of this.

There is something more, something deeper that I glimpsed briefly, when everything dissolved and I was standing in a field of pure potential. It looked like snow on an old TV screen. A blank slate? QUANTUM FOAM? I viewed it, I was it. It's not the first time I became foam but it definitely was the strongest and clearest.

This is the answer. For there to be no rules to reality one must embrace their own rules of reality. By embracing my own constructs I opened a doorway into being conscious of the field of pure potential, where I am a blank slate. Where I am truly free. I am sitting here at my kitchen table and I am simultaneously in that field of pure potential. No wonder I feel like I'm dissolving. It's taking over…

THE SECRET THAT WOULD HAVE KILLED ME

Here is the secret that would have killed me,
Slowly choking my senses
Into eternal dullness
With the promise of comfort,
The lure of escape
From the shame that is etched
Into the center of all my stories.

The secret exposed,

explodes.

And the blister separating me from myself

collapses

And I drop down
The steep surrender
Into the hollow echo of nothing.

My guts are dizzy,
My face is missing
And my heart is dust.
My legs are fossilized bone,
I smell unearthed stone
And I see the dull wood of old caskets.

Here I am clawing my way out of a sarcophagus.

Life is real again.

All that glitters is not gold. Some of us are not operating on the same frequency. My life has been marked by a great dilemma. One where I continuously choose intangibles over solid, measurable results. It's been a source of great uncertainty in my life. Yet there's a certainty that defies logic. I'm walking around with this question.

What really matters?

THE WEIGHT OF MY LIFE

I was doing a conscious witnessing meditation practice with a friend. During my time to share what I was feeling, gravity and intense pressure began pushing down on me. It was so heavy that I could barely stay in my chair. I just kept trying to describe it and feel into it and then I noticed that there was pressure from inside of me that was pushing out. Something inside of me was trying to get out. That something was who I really am. It was so soft and so subtle and yet I could feel it pushing so hard, like a baby fish breaking out of an egg. The part of me that flutters, the part of me that loves unconditionally, the part of me that is pure light and sensitivity was trying to birth itself. This was new. At that moment I understood so much. I saw all the moments in my life where I adopted a belief about how I needed to behave, or a belief about how the world is, all based on wanting to have this subtle part of me seen and honored. But the opposite occurred. Every one of those strategies on how to be in the world, all of them were tiny little weights, tiny little scales laid onto the truth of me. I felt the multitude of lead scales laid on my body like armor, covering the truth of who I really am. That is the "story" of my life and that is the weight of my life. But now the pressure inside was pushing the scales off. The pulsing inner light was showing the scales for what they were. I called out to my galactic family for reassurance and they came, I could feel their presence. My entire body was pulsing from the inside out, especially on the surface of my skin, like a strobing light, like a cuttlefish mesmerizing its prey. The sensation of strobing, pulsing light, pushing out the surface of my skin lasted for hours until I finally fell asleep. I woke up later and thought perhaps now I can become a real person. Without a story.

Awakening into form. What does that mean? It means your body is enhanced to the point that it becomes an expression of your self realization. It's more than that. It's your body waking up to its sacredness. The Sacred self is expressed through your physical form. Spirit meets flesh.

YOUR BODY BELONGS TO THE EARTH

Your body belongs to the earth, the elements, the seasons, to all of nature. All creatures have this in common, therefore all creatures dwell in you and you in them. Your body was meant for so much more than the island that harbors your soul. When you let go and imagine that you are all things, imagine the universe inside you, then you touch upon the truth about your body, what it can do and where it can go. You are not limited by the so-called physical. When you show up completely in your body, you disappear. The small self disappears and you become everything. Your body is The Way. Once you let go of your small ideas and let your imagination play freely, you can do anything. When you begin to let your body lead you'll be given great gifts that will heal you, give you strength, happiness, clarity and abundance. Come to that place where the still waters take you deep into yourself and you'll know you have arrived. Your body knows there is no time and there is no distance. As you open the portals to this awareness your body will heal itself because it lives beyond this dimension. Your body lives beyond this dimension.

REFRESHMENT

A new experience is now my food. My body is seeking refreshment from a new source of nourishment. I want to experience
what I don't yet know. That's all that's left to do. My body now
needs to be renewed every day. The body needs to be refreshed
in the present time. The body needs to have a new experience of
itself to feel refreshed. When this happens the gravity and weight
around my hips lifts up to a light bubble in my chest.

I AM BEING TAKEN OVER BY GENTLENESS

I am being taken over by gentleness. It's a warm breath that I draw deeply and slowly into me and as I do my whole world changes. I drop through ordinary reality into a vibrant, layered painting. As I exhale, I return to ordinary reality. Multidimensionality. This is it. There is no question that this is the new way. When I move in this new way it's as if I am walking through water. I can feel the gentle pressure flowing around me. I understand that the intense sense of gravity, the lethargy and fatigue was preparation, was my body getting ready to walk in this way of gentleness and ease. As long as I allow it and flow through that place of gentleness I am supported.

ARMOR PIERCING PUFFBALLS

Armor piercing puffballs,
Dandelion seeds,
Carrying their light codes
On the samsaric breeze.

If you think my tears are weak
You've got a lot to learn.
The legacy of the meek
Is about to take its turn.

ENJOY THE MIRACLE OF WHO YOU ARE

April 3, 2020, Covid Lockdown

The battle of dark and light has been brought to your doorstep. I'm not saying this is how it is but this is how it appears. The miracle of who you are embraces it all. Good, bad, dark, light, all of it is embraced with tenderness. Because you are all of it. And for me, when I stand in this place, your place and mine, there is no war and there never was. I stand on my doorstep and do my daily practice and expand in and out. I feel the sun on my skin and the wind on my face and I feel the massive awakening of humanity at this moment. What a time to be alive. Enjoy your inner treasures whatever they may be. This is the time. You have the time. Notice how many of us are cherishing each other, respecting each other and sharing the preciousness of life.

INNATE IS MAKING ART

My symptoms are my innate making art. What if the daily
aches and pains are my innate intelligence making art? What if
I stopped being afraid of it and became fascinated by what my
body can do? The colors of my pain. Pain is part of the poetry
of my existence, accompanied by the soundtrack of my angst.
Innate informs a cascade of thoughts, emotions and sensations
in continuous flux, each affecting the other. Walk around
in your wearable art. Living art that changes and morphs
throughout your day, always true, always you.

WHEN THE BODY TAKES OVER

There's been a sensation that has terrified me for many years. The terrifying sensation is losing control. I believe the mind is in control or to be more specific, I believe the mind is me and if the mind is not in control then I'm not in control. When the body takes over the mind loses control. Yet, there's an intelligence to the body, a multidimensional, innate intelligence that my mind cannot grasp. If I can feel the fear and breathe and relax into that sensation, it's not scary at all. It's the opposite of scary, it's an enhancement. I experience myself as more; more alive, more in love, more generous, more full, more everything. It's a departure from the limitations of the world as we know it. It's a departure from what I believe about myself. It's not easy to lose control, especially when it feels like the biological systems in place to keep me alive are detaching or unwinding from everything I know to be me. Am I dying? It does feel like a kind of death. I'm starting to see our inverted reality. What feels like death is moving into life. When I breathe and relax, the riches that are showing themselves to me, that ARE me, how could I be afraid of that? I now believe that's what the body is doing, it's leading me into another dimension of me.

EARTH ELEMENT IS CODES FOR CREATION

The physical body is the portal through which creation emerges. The body is of the earth. The codes for creation come from the earth element within you. Feel the freedom. Feel the blue sky inside you. Feel the majesty within every cell of your form. Earth element majesty. Grace, ease and serenity.

Can you feel the physical wind playing with your thoughts? Can you feel the wind playing with your desires? Is the physical wind inside of you? Is the wind moving through you? Of course it is. The world moves through you. You do not move through the world. So it's not about having physical strength and energy to move through the world. This is a deeply entrenched belief. It's more about floating or dancing. Perhaps it's about flowing. Perhaps it's about letting the deeper flow carry you.

POSTURE AND IMPOSTER

Every time I stand or sit or whatever position I take within my body, I hold a posture. Most of it is held by my subconscious beliefs. Beliefs I don't even know I'm holding about who I am in the world. So every time I notice and embrace the feelings and sensations of the posture that I'm holding, the more I see the imposter, the avatar, the limited identity that I present to the world. The more that I sense into and feel how I am standing and moving and why I am standing and moving in that way, I get to see a deeper intelligence coming up through the imposter, the deeper intelligence of my body that is authentic and real and alive in the here and now. I am coming to understand that being an imposter has been a tool necessary to navigate the linear world. Accompanying the sensation of being an imposter is self doubt. It's knowing that I'm not showing and sharing the magnificence of who I feel myself to be. Confusion follows about how to overcome this limitation and show up as who I really am. The answer is, it is not either/or. The quality of being an imposter may always be with me, in this life at least, but it doesn't have to be everything. In fact, there's more and more of just being a cosmic presence, a conscious presence and being quite satisfied with my own acknowledgment of self. It brings me back to that dream I had and that sentence that kept being repeated over and over, *"the gap between me and you is the gap between me and myself."* As long as I keep feeling myself when I'm around others there is no gap. When I allow myself to be in whatever state I am in I stop feeling like an imposter.

PUTTING ON MY SKIN SUIT

I envision it to be about 6 to 12 inches thick and it's made of a now-membrane that is partially energy and partially physical. When I put on my skin suit of *now-membrane* I come more fully into the present time. I experience more of myself and I feel the connection with all, the sounds around me, the tree in my view, all become a part of me. There's an ecstatic quality and also a quality of heaviness, dizziness and pain. The pain doesn't matter anymore because there's a knowing, an absolute assurance of cosmic law. I'm beginning to understand what my dizziness really is. I'm happy about it and grateful for it because I am going through a doorway! I'm a dizzy portal. So, in a way, I feel like a superhero or that I have a super power.

THE SHARPNESS OF THE KALEIDOSCOPE

The sharpness of the kaleidoscope is a part of me. It is me. I resisted the hard angles thinking that I needed to soften them but now I realize that the sensation of hard angles, of difficulty, of darkness even is all part of me and all are returning to me. If I am a portal then I am a kaleidoscope of all colors, all shapes, all angles, all qualities of experience, love, hate, strength, weakness, light, darkness, I am all of it and none of it. The more that I allow and accept and acknowledge, the stronger the sensation of return. It's all pouring into me. It's all pouring through me and the stronger the flow through me the more I can not hold onto any one thing. Nor do I want to. The flow is so satisfying. What a surprise.

TRUTHS THAT YOU FEEL

Truths that you feel

Are the truths that are real.

My body told me,

"You've always been on the right track".

I felt my hip and I felt my back.

All the self-doubt doesn't come

From the place where my Self comes from.

The dream place is where my Self comes from.

It's another day where I feel the energetic echoes running through my body. I feel the energetic signature of the celery that I ate a minute ago. I feel so sensitive, I can feel everything. It's a dizzying place, I feel weak and yet there is something, some strong thing running through me. For that I am grateful. What is taking all of my time and attention and energy, to where I am compelled to stop in the middle of my tasks and just take a deep breath and plunge inwardly, is an all-encompassing sensation that takes me down into myself and illustrates my insides with color, light and images. It's fascinating, it's beautiful and tender, quite tender. But what is this strong thing? I've been here so many times in the past and here I am again, being taken for a ride by the forces within me. And sometimes, briefly in one ecstatic moment I feel as if I am the one orchestrating this ride. I am the one designing it. I am the one molding it into my design. It's my creation. Though I can know this intuitively and intellectually there are brief periods when I am it. Those moments reassure me that I'm not dying; because it kind of feels like dying; that I'm not in decline but in fact I am claiming myself as the creator of my reality. I am stepping into creatorship.

THE FAMILIARITY OF THE UNKNOWN

How can this experience feel familiar when I've never had it before? Yet it does. Some part of me that I didn't know I had is recognizing it. The part of me that is part of something bigger is resonating with the unknown. Someone said that DNA is not a substance, it's an event. That's how this feels. This event, resonating with the unknown, I live for it. Some harmonic within me, perhaps it is my DNA, resonates and I know that I'm in the right place at the right time doing the right thing. From an outside observer this would look like nothing, but it's not nothing. I am soothed, comforted and encouraged to go on. Becoming familiar with the unknown inside is all I want to do. What a paradox.

LET YOURSELF DISAPPEAR

Let yourself disappear. I just heard this inside. Now I'm wondering, assuming that just like crystals, our bodies appear and disappear instantaneously. I'm wondering if all of the strangeness in my body, the heaviness, the lethargy, the dizziness, the bloating, the bleeding, if it all has to do with my body adjusting itself so that my body will give me a direct experience of disappearing and reappearing instantaneously. My next thought was, maybe that's what the pulse is. I feel the pulse often. Am I pulsing in and out of existence? It happens so fast that I perceive that I'm always here but that means I'm always not here as well. That voice wants me to go into the mystery, into nothing.

We keep behaving as if there are forces outside of us that can affect us. But the reality is that there is nothing outside of us except for what we project. The benevolent force is inside waiting to burst out so let it! An unfathomable, infinite source of life and creativity is inside waiting to burst forth. So let it.

SQUATTING IN THE CENTER OF THE GALAXY

Squatting in the center of the galaxy
In my victim pajamas.
It's so bright here
I can see right through them.
I can feel the warmth on my flesh.

Starting my day by
Resurrecting innocence.
Gathering all my catastrophes
       and weaving them
            into the brightness,
Like iridescent laces
Flecked with all the time capsules,
The history of human disasters
All running up my spine.
It's all mine.

Don't do what the old priests did
And crucify the one that will save you
With the doctrine of the sacred.

You don't know what is sacred.
That's where you stand.
          Innocent,

In the center of the galaxy
Reliving the resurrection
Every day.

STEP INTO YOUR LIGHT SUIT

Step into your light suit
And weave the rainbow bridge
With your rainbow footprints.
With your rainbow eyes.
The bridge is all our freedom.
Bridge across the sky.

THE ADOLESCENT SHELF

That's where childhood wounds got locked away, put away, hidden. It's the modern coming of age ritual. Instead of a ceremony with all the elders present, honoring your emergence into adulthood, you get to hide away from everyone. There, alone in your room, you place the innocence of your youth in a dark corner somewhere where no-one ever sees. That's the adolescent shelf. I can see it and feel it inside of me. I finally landed here after a long, long fall. Do not fear the fall, do not fear the dropping into the caverns of your catastrophes. Now I can be the elder to my adolescent. I can be with her and she can feel the comfort of my gaze and my knowing embrace. Now I can visit and reclaim my body, reclaim the health of my body as all the hidden wounds are healed; as all the programming, to carry impossible, back breaking burdens, is released. All my timelines are brought into this now-moment and my past is rewritten.

CHUCK YOUR PRIDE

Chuck your pride, you won't die, chuck your spiritual materialism and you'll be free. No-one knows what's coming. No-one. Not knowing is so deeply embedded into natural law that it is the zero point. Not knowing is the point of conception. So whatever experiences you need to set up to shatter your spiritual pride, bring them on. You'll find the thing that you thought was helping you is actually keeping you from being free; free to enjoy all the support and all the aspects of your multidimensional self who are rising up and assembling to give you the most profound experience of awakening. It's happening now. Emerging through you now are all of the experiences that happened before thought, experiences that happened outside of time. All of those experiences give you a new framework to lay your beliefs upon. You are transitioning from the old beliefs about spirituality into a new idea of awakening into multidimensionality. Your mind will come to understand what is happening.

I've been asking for this for about 10 years. My resistance is wearing down. The body's wisdom is starting to take over. The body's wisdom, beyond my personality, beyond my intellect, beyond anything I can conceive of, this sensation that I don't have control of and it's a sensation of… wellness? I really can't explain it but I sure am loving it. First pass of the self-driving body is everything in my immediate vicinity becomes semi liquid and I can see and sense the ripples, like the ripples of light you see at the bottom of a pool. Everything is made of this rippling energy and then everything in my immediate vicinity is me. It's a part of me. The deck that I'm standing on, the stairway that's leading up to my deck, I sense it as a part of me. I'm coming to understand that this is how I'm creating it. Within my body there is a sense of primacy, something I don't know if I've ever experienced before. My body is the primary driver, not the person that I believe myself to be. Accompanying the sense of primacy it is a deep understanding that all is well. All the things I was concerned about are not really an issue; those issues are elusive, illusory and impermanent. The body is the center of everything. This is not the body as we have known it. This is a center of intelligence, far more intelligent than the programmed mind. The body knows all.

I suddenly glimpsed that lifeforce exists, dwells outside of our creations. We imbue our creations with life when we believe them into being. We do it unconsciously and then we believe we are at the affect of our creations. We live out a timeline based on our creations. Inverted reality. We tether ourselves to our creations without knowing we are doing it. What if we could feel the mechanisms by which we create our reality? Which are not mechanisms, they are a biological process. A life process.

YOU ARE ALL THAT MATTERS

An aspect of me, a toddler, stepped into my living room today and I felt myself as her, felt how tenuous and uneasy she was, how unsure she was of herself. When I said the words, "you are all that matters," I opened the door to a part of me that had been locked out of my awareness. The part of me that was searching for what matters. Searching everywhere for what matters because I was shown and I believed, deep in my heart, that I didn't matter.

All those aspects of myself who were not cherished are returning. Cherishing becomes a natural act, like breathing, impossible to stop for long, impossible to not feel. Cherishing is freed from exchange, from the framework of transaction. You cannot earn being cherished. You just are. Hidden treasures are being returned. Parts of me that were encapsulated and kept safe are opening. Embrace what is hidden and you may find a treasure. Treasures outside of belief. I am a treasure outside of belief. By embracing my limited identity I build a bridge to my unlimited identity. My unlimited identity is speaking to me with the language of sensation, the common language that connects the limited material form with unlimited multidimensional awareness.

Go back in time and find yourself as an infant. Was there hunger, isolation, confusion, anguish? Hold yourself and say, "you are all that matters." Feel it echo through all time. Find the original encapsulation of your spirit. like a jewel that you kept on a chain around your neck. Understand what the hunger was for and understand what the need was for. See the treasure, a gift you've been waiting to give to yourself, the thing that you needed most that you didn't know that you needed. Bring that love starved infant into the light. Feel the wide, deep hollow; the vast emptiness inside your tiny little belly. This is the part of you you are speaking to. Now say; "you are all that matters, you are all that matters, you are all that matters."

When your beloved little one appears, she gives you the thing that you didn't even know you needed.

The new flavor of sovereignty is being the sculptor of your reality. The new flavor of sovereignty is recognizing that everything else is a sideshow. The biggest sideshow of all is your identity. The one you spent your life cultivating and curating. Do the sovereign dance, sculptor of reality. Lose yourself in the movement until you find yourself, gasping with delight, in a place you've never been before.

THE BODY GOES ROUND AND ROUND

The body goes round and round in a circle of how you feel. The body goes round and round, throwing out realities in a perfect circle that comes back to you, like iridescent bubbles that float up briefly and then pop as they land on your face. And you think, what was that? Why did that happen? Because you blew life into it, that's why. That's all, there is nothing else. Here I am, a human of the realm and what else? Am I what you tell me I am? I don't think so but feel free to tell me. I don't have to negotiate with your ideas about me anymore. I don't have to negotiate with my own ideas about me anymore. I'm a perfect circle. I'm a brief circle of containment for what cannot be contained. I am a brief glimpse of majesty and then it's gone.

PAPER BOATS

This morning I saw myself making little paper boats. All my life
I've been folding paper boats and putting them into the water
and watching them float away. They only last for a while until they
become soft with water, sink and dissolve into the current. All
my life I felt like a failure because my little paper boats became
nothing. But this morning I realized that making little paper boats
and watching them float away is the only thing that I want to do.
My boats don't become nothing. They become everything. So if
you come across a soggy little boat, a semi-dissolved dream, a
message without a bottle, a water-logged wish washed up at your
feet, know who sent it.

I've been having experiences of connecting with myself without an identity. I experience my form as colors, shapes and sounds, quite vivid and beautiful. There is an intensity of feeling but without the persona. It's quite disorienting, I am quite lightheaded and yet I feel that this is the way. While I'm in this state I can still talk and think. My body keeps taking this big, deep. full body breath, like a deep sigh and I feel almost as if I'm breathing underwater. My diaphragm opens up, my chest opens up and there's a thickness to the breath, like being in the womb and breathing the amniotic fluid. Is this how I am being reborn into multidimensionality? But the main thing that has my curiosity peaked is when my identity appears to me as a little wisp of code. My identity is like an adornment. I can wear it or not.

Just before I fell asleep, I sensed a truth in my body and now I can't remember what it was. It was such a profound realization and so powerful and a moment later I couldn't remember it. But since my body had gotten it, my cells had registered it, I just relaxed and fell into a really bizarre kind of sleep where I was not really asleep.

I remember, while I was laying there, achy and feverish and weak, that my body was telling me it was slowing me down on purpose. My body was speaking in a very loud volume. All of my symptoms and complaints, they're very loud, they take up all my attention and energy and I don't like it. I've been really trying to negotiate with my body to calm down so that I could go out and play but my body said, *"No, you need to just be still and pay attention to me. Be still and protect me all day long, every day until I tell you that we're done and we're not done yet."* Maybe that was the realization; stop trying to negotiate. My body was shouting, *"pay attention!"* My body was shouting louder than the experienced and knowledgeable healer, Micah Lee Malloy, L.AC. LMT, etc, etc. who was going through her mental catalog of causes and remedies to find a solution to my pain. My body was answering, with less than quiet intensity, *"be still. Just. Be. Still."*

I surrendered. Something let go. That was the profound release. I let go of everything I know about healing. Which is a lot. A big part of my identity is wrapped up in what I know about healing. Once I did that, curled up in my bed, my body took over healing me. That's why my sleep didn't feel like sleep. That's why, even though I'd been trying to take different supplements, essential oils and herbs to help with my symptoms, my body was just revolting. It doesn't want anything to treat my condition, my body wants to envelop, embrace and emerge with my conditions, with my symptoms. My body has got its own way of healing. And even that word, healing, seems like a very mistaken idea. The idea that there's something that needs to be balanced, harmonized, fixed or repaired. This is not the case. My mind doesn't understand it. Everything that I've learned about anatomy, physiology and alternative medicine, it just doesn't apply anymore. All I can do is be still, breathe and feel and let my body show me the way.

FROM DIZZY SPELLS TO PRESENCE SPELLS

Dizzy spells do pull you into the present moment really quickly, don't they? What if that's the intention? What if that's the design? A reorientation into the awareness of formlessness, the awareness of a non-fixed reality? The old programming says I must be sick, there must be something wrong, but I'm not so sure! Maybe there's just something new, something so new that there's no reference for it. Your neurology, your physiology reacts just as it would if you suddenly found yourself in a completely new place than where you were a second before. The dizziness is a loss of weight, a loss of pressure. The moment that precedes the dizziness is often a spontaneous stretch, a deep stretch that starts deep in my core, pushing my physicality, pushing my physiology, pushing my biology beyond the veil. And the spontaneous sounds that come out of me, the toning, the humming, that's the sound of emergence. When the sound and the sensation merge in resonance it's my physiology expressing its freedom, expressing its emergence out of limitation.

MY PERSONALITY IS A PASSENGER

My innate intelligence will take me through whatever releases are necessary, be it emotional, physical, whatever. That is my new vibrational reality. In other words, the innate intelligence of my body that is connected to Natural Law, Cosmic Law is now driving and my personality is a passenger.

I was standing and I stretched my arms, like a cat, arching my back, sticking my chest out and it felt like I was going to fall down. Then all these particles of light were pouring out of my chest like I created an electromagnetic pulse. The kaleidoscope has softened, the kaleidoscope is integrating into my biology, into my physicality, into my physiology. That's how it feels. The stretching happens spontaneously, like my innate body is reaching for the light.

TODAY I GOT SO CLOSE TO MY BROKEN HEART

Today I got so close to my broken heart that I could feel the poison in my veins. This poison formed my life. It was the ink from which I was drawn. This pain shaped the contour of my reality. In this moment of reckoning I can not escape it. The time of running from this feeling is over. I believed that I was an outsider, that I didn't belong in my family, in my human family or in the world. And then, because I reached the bottom of my pain, it flipped. I saw myself inside of everything. I am the center of the family. I am the connection. I am sacred. Now I can feel the fabric of my world tearing open. I can feel how my body makes the world. I am free.

MOST OF THE FEELING IN MY BODY IS AN ECHO

Most of the feeling in my body is an echo. It is not in the present time. But when I sensed eternity, that was my nervous system in connection with present time, in connection with the plasma field. I was having a direct experience of eternity, of my eternity, of the eternalness of me.

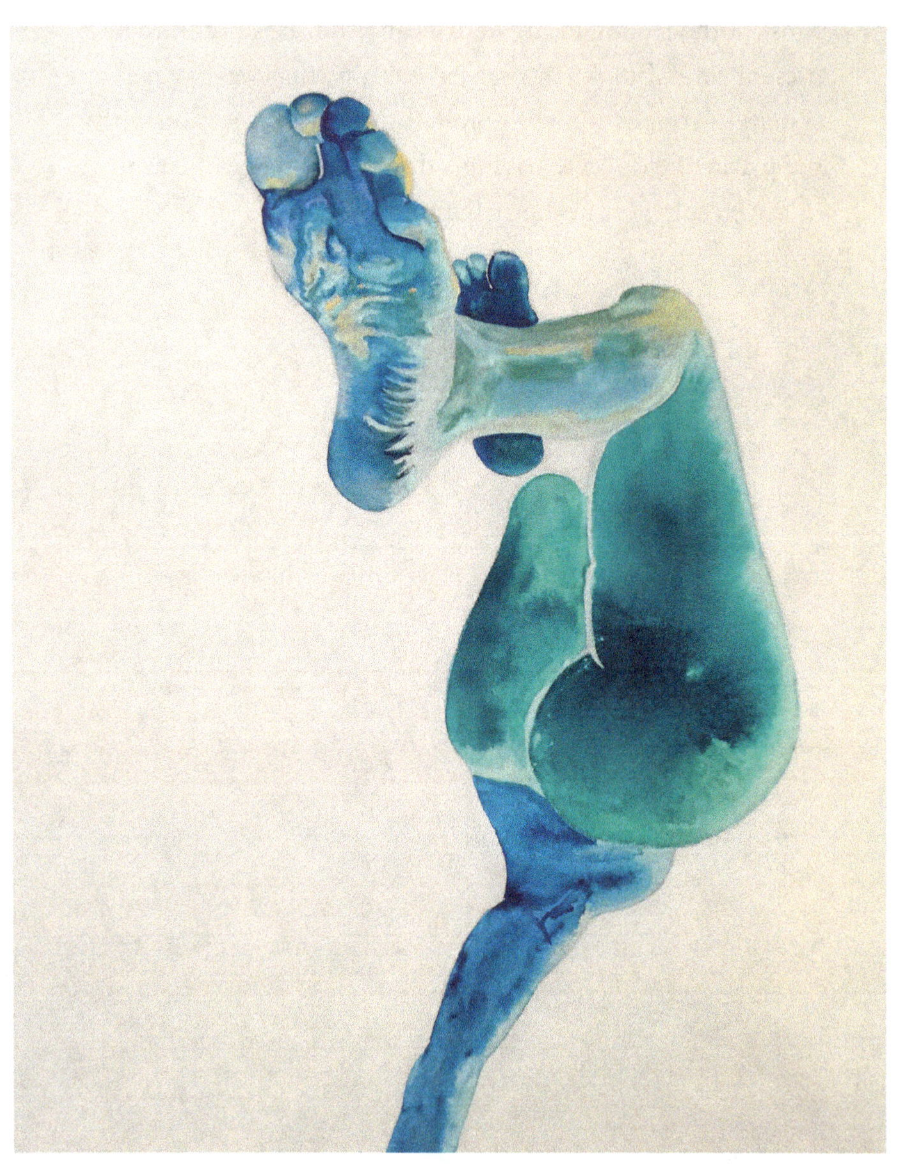

EARTH GRAVITY VERSUS COSMIC GRAVITY

I have so many questions about earth's new position in space and the consequences for humanity. Cosmic gravity is coming into alignment with earth's gravity. Is that why we've all been experiencing so much heaviness? Because our consciousness is now becoming aware of the earth's gravity? The resistance, the friction, the heaviness feels like it's a shell, a brittle coating that lies atop my skin or lies atop my energy field. My intuition is to just keep continuing to embrace the shell as a mode of coming more and more into alignment with cosmic gravity. Is my incessant fatigue the body saying, *"you're acting against cosmic constancy, you are going against the grain."* I just had this experience again where my body was self-driving, my feet were self-driving in a way that was directly from my innate intelligence; pre-persona movement. Is this moving with cosmic gravity? I have an idea that all of the physical exertion that is so familiar, that I quite love and I'm grieving the loss of, all exertion is based on being in the resistance to cosmic gravity. So, I'm hoping that at some point I achieve the level of integration where I can play physically, hike, ride my bike and surf in harmony with cosmic gravity.

BEING UNDEFENDED

Any place where I'm defended needs to fall away, drop away. Because all those defenses are going against the grain of natural law. I'm getting some pretty intense assistance from others in this falling away process. My defenses are showing up in high contrast, which isn't easy for me. It appears to me in the form of other people's defenses. Others are being defensive and it's getting in my way, and hurting my heart. But are they? Is it them who are being defensive or is it me projecting my defensiveness onto them? Or is it a combination? How do I register the incongruity of what someone is saying to me with what I feel from them? Mostly, it's some kind of unease that I detect. But they don't admit it. Then I get suspicious and uneasy. Stuff doesn't match. It rarely matches. Is there an easier way to connect with my own unease, staying true to myself? It's OK to not be OK. I have said this so many times to myself and others. I am remembering the sensation that I had for five days after Mom died where all of my discomfort and unease was such an afterthought. It was there but it had no effect on me because I was so deeply and profoundly in touch with my eternalness.

Being with my family at the funeral in the way that I was, so grateful to be with my siblings, appreciating them while being in the wash of grief and all of the family drama, the emotions and all the history, this was new for me and it was a great power. My experience at the funeral was an introduction to how to be in the world, how to be social. I feel like I'm being propped up by white light.

SELF WORTH

When my mind goes blank
the fear is,

well...

I have finally achieved

becoming a complete

zero.

TO LOVE THE PAIN

I am starting to love the pain because it's mine, it's not a mistake, it's not an error. There isn't something wrong with me. It is me. And it is you. I love your pain too. I cannot separate from myself. Why would I want to? It's mine. I claim this land and every dark river, every deep unknown. It's mine. I'm giving birth to myself.

THE POOL

I had a dream that I was looking after three little girls, so I took them to the pool. They all jumped into their lanes, like baby ducks to water and started swimming. Then I got into the pool but there was no clearly marked lane for me. I didn't know what the rules were for the pool! I was trying to figure out where to go when this woman came up to the pool and started flirting with me. "You must be a world-class swimmer," she said, "you obviously really know what you're doing." I said no, I have no clue. I was looking up at this well-dressed, not unattractive woman who was clearly out of my league, considering whether to flirt back, when I heard the whisper of a thought, barely perceptible, that she was not even close to what I want but I would probably go for it anyway. Then I woke up. While I am having my coffee and starting my day, my predominant thought is, I want somebody who's already in the pool.

THE SOUND OF GOLD

Recently, when hanging out with a friend, I heard myself speaking. It felt more like the larger me, an aspect of me that is beyond my personality, was hearing me speak. The sound of my voice felt golden, it felt like a treasure. It's a new blending of senses. I have seen and felt gold, light and many treasures when I massage a client. I have seen and felt veins of gold inside of myself. But I have never heard it before. This is a sound. My sound feels golden. Interestingly, this morning my ears are plugged!

SOME OF THE BUILDING BLOCKS OF ME
ARE MADE OF PAIN

Pain is life force. My life force. If pain is part of my foundation then I must be in agreement with it in order to feel stable. In order to feel completely safe I must know all of my building blocks. I see them rising up from beneath me, showing themselves to me, some of them shadowy, some of them murky and yet they are mine so I don't need to be afraid. Another part of me, maybe the larger part of me is saying, *"it's OK look at this and feel this within you. Greet this part of you, embrace it."* Even in this shadowy, murky pain there is a blessing. The blessings of pain.

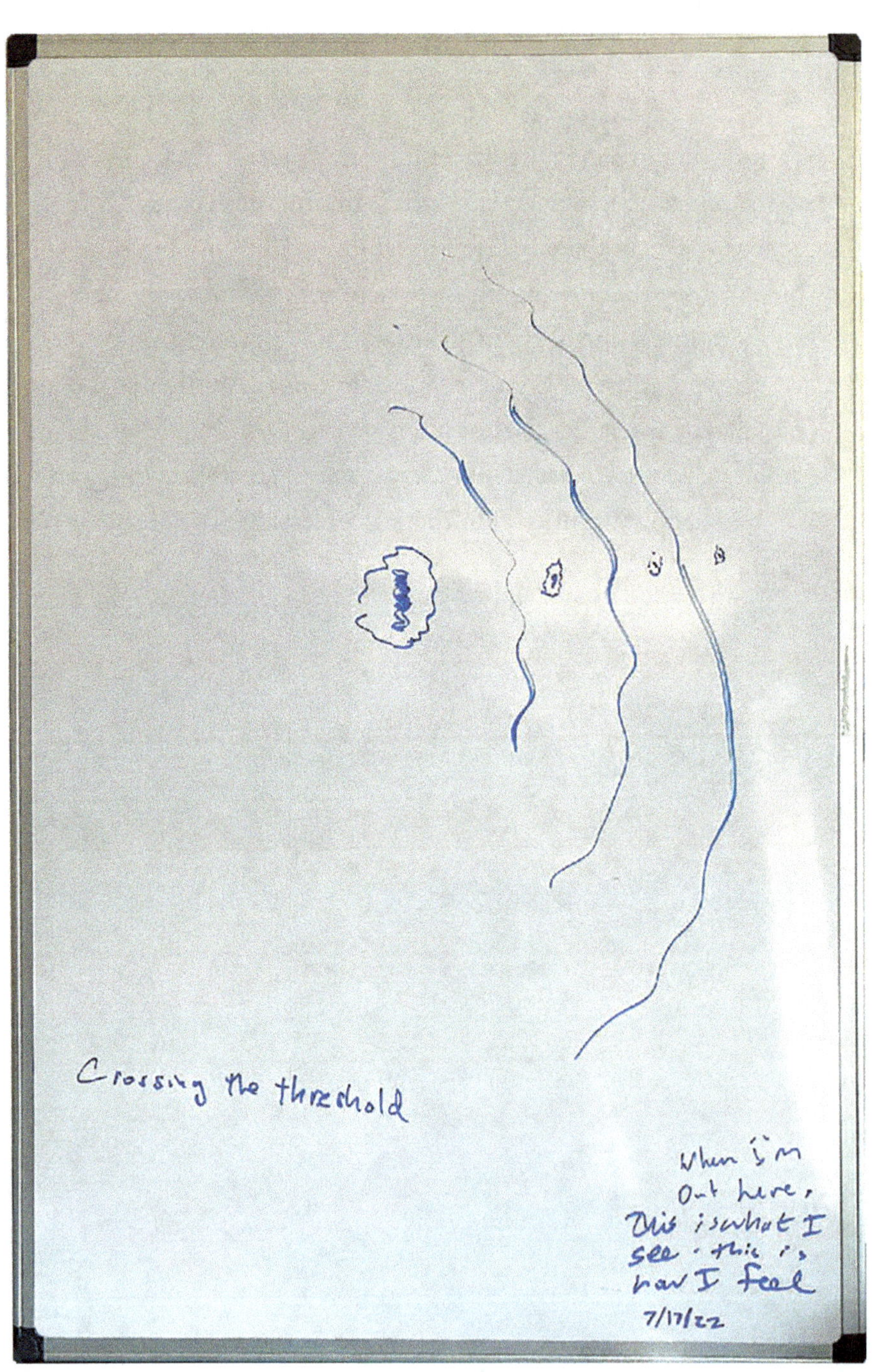

Crossing the threshold
When i'm out here, this is what I see. this is how I feel
7/17/22

During my practice I saw this image. What I was being shown is that there are certain states where I can easily cross into the non-physical, non-material, the imaginal realm and its full potency. The potency of realization and creativity. Often when I am in one of these states I don't feel so stable and strong. I feel weak. The image is showing me that it's not weakness, it's just a sensation of being able to leap dimensions. The Vision is showing me that it's a gift.

I am not so identified with being a physical body. My body becomes a bit of dust. My body becomes a squiggle. No, that's not it. Something larger is viewing what I thought my body was and from this larger perspective it looks like a bit of a squiggle. My thought is the squiggle. All my thinking that I'm dying or thinking that I'm not well is because I'm not fully claiming my body. What if something larger is claiming my body? What if I'm becoming more than that little bit of thought? I am becoming more than everything that I thought I was and everything that I thought I was looks pretty small and not even symmetrical. It's just a squiggle. I wanna turn myself into something more.

If I have this opportunity as a creative generator to alchemise all of the disconnection, then everyone that I meet, who is actually a part of me, I have the opportunity to bring them all back into connection. I'm here unwinding the belief in disconnection, the belief that we are separate and apart from each other. The big heart-breaking beliefs. The ones everyone, almost, accept as just the way things are. I become a wave of thought-forms. These giant waves of thought forms wash over me and through me as I allow them. I am them. That's the only way to fully alchemise separation is to recognize that I am all these beliefs of separation. When I do that I see and feel that I am more than that. I am the liquid, the membrane, the plasma that holds it all together. I'm all of it. All the different flavors of separation that are offered by my child, my friends, strangers, I am feeling it all and my heart does feel broken. Am I to let the emotion run through me,? Am I to feel the pain? It's better to feel the pain, it's better to let it pass through me. It isn't fun and it isn't easy but as the pain passes through me I do feel more ease and more spaciousness and peace. And my body feels better. I'm seeing that all of the impressions of separation that I have don't have to put me in a box. It's an opportunity to feel the pain and open to the larger truth that there is no separation. In fact, the reason that I'm feeling pain is because separation is a lie. The heartbreak is because my heart knows the truth. If anyone is offering an impression of separation and I don't receive it as such, then I've provided the alchemy for that moment. I'm having great compassion right now for this little human who has walked through a lifetime of separation and who is facing even more intense grief as I pass through this alchemical doorway, not knowing what's on the other side. I am at another threshold experience

THIS MOVEMENT, THIS EXPRESSION

This movement, this expression is such a beautiful thing and this is not a little thing. This is not a little thing. So don't let your thinking diminish the meaning of what you are becoming. Don't let your thinking diminish the meaning of what you're creating. Continue to listen to the sensations and the images and the sounds that are moving you, expressing and revealing your embodiment of your divinity, embodiment of your multidimensionality. Embodiment of love. Because that's what this is. It's not a little thing. It's not a little dance. It's not a little stretch. Don't worry how it looks from the outside. Inside is outside. Keep repeating, inside is outside and forget about winning anybody over ever again. Don't bow to someone else's pretense. Those days are over. Don't let your beliefs about being minimized and being disregarded be the whole truth. Embrace your history of being rejected and disregarded. Embrace it, it's part of the fabric of this new creation that's coming through you. Embrace it and it will no longer have power over you, compelling you to behave in ways that do not reflect the truth of who you really are. You can't really win anyone else over with this. This is just for you and the more that you let it be just for you the more it becomes for everyone else. Follow the sensation of the movement, the sensation of the movement, the sensation of the movement. Not the purpose, not the motive, not the outcome. The becoming of the movement. Eventually your innate intelligence, dwelling within every cell of your body, becomes the driver of this magnificent vessel that is your body. Then, natural law becomes your dance partner. Universal law becomes your playground. The joy of being becomes your supply, the standing wave that you ride upon.

I'M SOMEONE WHO ANSWERS

I'm someone who answers

Your questions before they are asked.

I'm still looking for a pat on the head

But soon I think that will pass.

Maybe this feeling doesn't need to be judged and fixed. Maybe this is the feeling of fresh new leaves still moist with their unfolding. Maybe this is the feeling of unfolding a new leaf imbued with your energetic signature. Ask for something in nature to show you where you are. Ask for something living in your environment to show you where you are. Because everything that you see is a reflection of your internal environment. Therefore, what you see will give you clear clues into where you are at. Eventually what you see in your "external" environment will be an affirmation, so look for things that affirm you, look for things that have a sign and have a message for you. The nature of nature is that it is here to serve you and show you the real you.

POSSIBILITY

We live in a field of possibility. This is more than a concept
although the conceptualization and the imagination are definitely part of it. But the field of possibility is all around you
right now. It's in the air that you breathe and on the surface
of your skin. It's inside of your cells. It's always touching you.
You're swimming in it. The idea that things and objects and
people are solid and outside of you is just that. It's an idea. It's
a belief. You are so powerful that you bring that belief into the
reality that you experience moment by moment and day by
day. You make it so. It seems like it's the belief that has power
over you but it's actually the reverse. You have all the power
and you always have had all the power. If the field of possibility that is with you right now, touching you right now had a
fragrance, how would it smell? If it had a flavor how would it
taste? And if it had a sensation, how would infinite possibility
feel? Do you see where this is going? It's what you make of it.
But that's not the whole picture because there is an element
of the unknown that always accompanies your new creation.
That's why it's called possibility.

RIDE THE PAIN

Ride the pain
Into the silence.
Ride the silence into source.

When I find bits and pieces, leftover attachments to who I
was trying to be, or to what I was trying to overcome, now
I see something that does not serve but only diminishes my
perfection. It's a gift to be emancipated from all those things
that tied me to the old reality. I can no longer be in the
reality that made me small and insignificant, yet even that
serves me. Because when I truly accept being nothing, then
I become everything. In the silence I welcome the wisdom
of others who are crossing the threshold, who are crossing
the veil, who are living in the subtle energy. I can see now
how hard I tried to make one single thing work in 3-D but
nothing did. There's nothing left to try to be in tiny 3-D
anymore. There's nothing to limit me anymore. Something's
so unreal about these words, they don't feel like they're living
in me anymore. Silence and stillness live in me now. Emancipation from my daughter forced me into silence. There's
nothing I can say, there's nothing I can do but nod and agree
and say OK, I shall return to myself.

PAINT ME WITH LINES OF GOLD

Paint me with lines of gold,

In the darkest places,

Where there is no landscape,

Where the ground is waiting to take its shape,

Pushed up by the unseen forces

Moving the earth beneath my feet.

Paint my insides with veins of liquid light,

Solid no more.

If you knew how softly you were held, how tenderly you were kissed by nature, you wouldn't fear a thing. When my footsteps sink into new domains, my feet are telling me I'm standing on a new plane, a new plateau. My feet can tell me much about the real world. My feet can show me the new way. My feet are making puddles. And the puddles are cuddles from the earth.

EVERYTHING YOU KNOW ABOUT YOUR BODY

Everything you know about your body is just the cover of the book. It's a two dimensional or three-dimensional representation of what's inside. You were never meant to be deaf, dumb and blind to the innate intelligence inside of your body. Your innate intelligence does so much more than keep your heart beating and your lungs breathing and your blood circulating and your nervous system firing. Your innate multidimensional operating system is your access to all wisdom. All truths. It is your access to co-creating reality.

What we know about the body is about 1% of what's really going on.

What we know about the body is such a crude representation of the elegance, sophistication, and pure magic of what the body really is. I'm curious to find out how many of us are interested in being in the unknown of the body. The mystery of the body. That's my quest.

The body is more like a blank canvas but not a three-dimensional canvas, more like a plane of existence. And on this plane, we are constantly writing, drawing, painting, expressing, dancing. My experience is that this is deeply, inherently personal. All of the drawing and writing and such comes through me as me. My question is, why is everyone pretending it's not? Do you see how crucial this understanding is? When everyone begins to recognize that their entire world is a deeply personal reflection of who they are, what a birthday party that will be. What a silly, joyful, stark naked revelation that will be.

SLEEPWALKING TOWARDS DESTINY

Sleepwalking towards my destiny,

A gift appears at my feet,

Unwraps its ribbons of whimsy,

And a miracle pops out,

Picks up my body

And twirls me in a whirlwind of delight.

The new meaning of twisting in the wind.

All my smarts are gone.

What's left is a mind exploring sensation.

What's left is a mind guided by imagination.

Let it take you.

Let it dance you.

There's nowhere to go and everywhere to be.

PRESSURE

I'm curious about the pressure, heaviness and gravity many of us are feeling every day.

Imagine a pearl forming deep in the darkness, in the folds of an oyster's body, under a mountain of water. That's us right now. I'm really curious about this water pressure. I'm wondering if the water in me can make me liquid enough that I feel the pressure but I'm free to move through it. I am imagining the wall of water the Masters were describing. They said the liquid inside of us is how we portal to other dimensions. Is it how we portal in and out of form? We are doing it all the time without knowing we are doing it.

If you become involved in the narrative that is our 3D reality, you become a caricature in the cartoon. All of the humanitarian agendas have been usurped by a small group of individuals whose interest is only to control you. Some examples are stewarding the earth, gay rights, women's rights and racial equality. All of these movements are now a controlled narrative run by billionaire interests. And their interests are not your interests. Their interests are to keep you playing this game of being disempowered, helpless and looking outside yourself for the answers. The answers are not outside of you. You are the answer. There is enough power in one tree to scrub the air and balance the soil, more than enough to light an entire city. If one tree has that much power imagine how much power you really have.

SHAMANIC JOURNEY

A Shamanic journey is when you go into non-ordinary reality to find answers or guidance from the magical, natural realm. Usually your first journey is to travel to the Lower World. To enter the lower world, you find an opening in the earth or a knot in a tree, or some kind of opening that takes you down there. I had the thought that I could descend to the lower world through the pain in my back. Any kind of pain in your body is like that, it's a hole in the Earth. It's a crease that can take you into non-ordinary reality if you let it. I also had the thought that non-ordinary reality is multidimensionality. Then I got excited and curious about the unknown adventure I was about to go on. A journey away from what I know about my pain into what could be. There's a sense of acknowledgment and affirmation, a sense of power. There's something really important about this practice.

I also had the impression of breathing underwater. A shamanic journey can also begin by entering water. Navigating third dimensional reality while being in a multidimensional state is a bit like breathing underwater. It's like being in ordinary reality and non-ordinary reality at the same time. It's like learning to breathe underwater. The thickness of source energy can be accessed with your lungs with deliberate, slow, deep breaths. There's been an ongoing and continuous encroachment into what used to be ordinary reality. There's a feeling that it's not real, that the artificiality and the lack of depth, the superficiality of ordinary reality is getting more and more apparent. My old habit was to become superficial myself to fit in. What I'm being shown is while I'm being a three dimensional creature to continue to breathe the source energy into me and maintain awareness of my multidimensionality. Every now and then I get this glimpse of myself. I'm seeing myself from my larger self and the impression I have of myself is that I am exquisite, just exquisite. So I have a sense that this is coming for me, to perceive everyone and everything with this larger view. You are the treasure, you are the fruit, you are the jewel. I think that's the revolutionary state, being both form and formless. The way of the shaman is to blend realities with the assistance of the natural realm.

What's coming out of my mouth now is full of whimsy. I can see it. No need to connect with all of the trappings of the old, tired paradigm. This is a whole new way of being deliberate. There are a lot of ways to be deliberate about sharing. One of them is whimsical. One of them is heartfelt and sincere. One of them is spontaneous and authentic. I can see what's happening, I am letting go of the old programming. I am trying not to cast the old spells, not trapping myself in the old lexicon of limitation. The new spells, they're just full of light and whimsy. Or they're from the heart and they are tender. Almost too tender to share. That's how I know. A new definition of sacred or sacredness appears and disappears without a trace. The mind asks, *"What was that? Wow! Something sacred just happened!"*

The words are on a roll. They have a life of their own. They make me smile as they come out of my mouth. They make my heart so happy that I almost feel like crying. Freedom.

My cooling kettle creaks in the kitchen as the night's chill tries to retake the room. But the morning sun promises warmth. I sit at my table and feel Providence taking its claim on me. My wild and savage imagination is walking a path through giant crystal skyscrapers that shimmer and sparkle and cast no shadow. My native land. I am home.

All your perfectly malleable mistakes turn into greeting cards. Embossed with the lyric that moves in all directions at once. Nothing can be captured. It's just for the moment. You know what comes next? This moment never ends, that's what comes next. Escape linearity.

You can't be everything until you accept that you are the lowest common denominator of your longing. When you embrace that you are every dark thing that you have ever imagined, you start to see how you created them. When you see the building blocks of reality then you know that you have arrived in the place where you are becoming everything. You're not afraid to be anything. You're not afraid to be the lowest of the low. You're not afraid of pain. You're not trying to be anything different than what you are.

THERE IS NO CONSEQUENCE

There is no consequence to your actions because our reality is inverted. Forget about instant manifestation.

It's the vibration that has the power. I can sense and feel the power in this vibration and I can sense and feel the unwinding and releasing of the fear programming. There is a thread of fear, the thread of fear that says there is something very wrong with you. If you're awash in vibration, you're either sick or dying. But this state is actually bearing witness, being inside of the power, the power of the vibration. Again, it's inverted because being in the power of the vibration initially feels like the opposite, it feels like powerlessness. It feels like I can't act. *"Oh my God, I am overwhelmed by this sensation of dissolving."* But, in truth, I've dropped into the pole position. I have my hand on the lever and I am finally steering. I've dropped into the power of the vibration. Then, when I realize that I am in power, I get excited and my emotion shifts from fear and doubt to curiosity and awe. The vibrational state hasn't changed but emotion has and that makes all the difference. When I'm afraid that there's something very wrong I can't act, I can't move, I curl up in a ball.

I imagine dropping into my vibration, becoming form and formless at the same time and in this place accessing the vibrational matrix of what I want to manifest. This is the singularity. This is the place of potentiality and potentializing. I can see now that I have used this state in the past to take action because of the excitement and the curiosity that I felt. I was devoid of fear and apprehension. But I keep having this thought that the manifestation doesn't even matter, it's being in this vibrational state, that is where I want to be. Because whatever I manifest is an illusion! This is too funny. My mind is completely blown.

IS POTENTIAL A SUBSTANCE?

I spent hours today in stillness, witnessing. Now there's something with me, a non-physical substance that got produced because I spent a great deal of time in the here-and-now listening to my body, feeling my body. It's like a spiritual escrow. It feels like wealth. I didn't have much choice to be in stillness because I felt so strange and not in a good way. I did not feel well. As I witnessed myself, I came closer and closer to these very subtle perceptions of myself. The more subtle, the more powerful. I kept holding space for the subtle aspect of me which I felt was potential. My mind kept wanting to make it into something and I just kept letting go and going back to pure potential. It was really difficult. But fruitful. Expansive.

WITHIN YOUR WATERS

Fear not

    what lies deep within your waters

The unfillable hole

    awaits your presence.

My spine isn't a spine at all.

    It's a series of windows.

        It's a ladder made of portals.

Pain in my belly woke me up at midnight. I was asking God, why do I have to feel this pain? I found myself in a place I have never been before. I realized that I was asking myself this question. I was pleading with the part of myself that I believe is God. Of course it's me. It's the creative part of me. I am creating this experience. The creative part of me is not who I think I am. It's not a part of me I can identify or hold on to. But I can talk to the creative part of me. I can listen to the Creator. I can hear the creator inside me, saying, "Just feel the sensation. Don't try to figure it out, just feel the sensation, just be with the sensation." I sat in the sensation of being a victim of my pain and helpless to change the pain, the intensity of which I never felt before, and I was calm. I just laid there and was with it. I was feeling the weight of being human. I can feel it in my cells. This is what I am drawing back into me. No more fighting it. I feel so blessed right now, it doesn't make any sense.

It's the hidden part of the iceberg that I am melting. We use up so much of our energy maintaining everyday reality where we are separate from the creative aspect of ourselves. That's why our lives are so short. The larger part of ourselves, the creative part, is like the massive foundation of the iceberg that is hidden below the ocean. Imagine carrying that iceberg around your whole life. Not acknowledging it. Doing your best to pretend it's not there with your belief and your programming. It's so overwhelmingly cold and deep and dense and scary. Who would want to feel that? This goes back to the very beginning of this writing where I was asking the creator why do I have to feel this? Interesting that it's water. It's frozen but then it thaws. All that's been held there gets released into the ocean. It might be ice, but it's just water waiting to thaw. I'm thinking of the meditation of the golden flame inside. Melting the ice inside. I'm having an image of me, the creator, keeping this giant ice cube frozen until finally the force of nature inside me, the flame inside me begins to melt it. It's my consciousness, but it's more than my consciousness. It is me, and it's beyond me.

My body is a bundle of feelings. Feelings which can't be stopped. Perhaps it is the reason for the deep weakness in my back and body, because I can not accept that my body is actually a bundle of feelings. My body is more a bundle of feelings than it is anything else. I am reviewing all of the programming I've had that feelings are elusive, like clouds, or like vapors, they come and they go. Feelings amount to nothing. It gives me a great sense of weakness in my body. I am nothing but a fleeting wisp of smoke. Also, in this ongoing process of realizing and accepting the illusory nature of my existence, my physiology would reflect that in some way. It has been reflecting that for many years as I reassemble my physiology into something that is beyond what I've been taught. As I ascribe to the doctrine of the unknown, I am making peace with being a contradiction.

This world may be built on ideas, but the next world is built on feelings.

CODEPENDENCE

Another middle of the night realization. It's about my mother and my daughter. It's about the way I was raised and the way I raised my daughter. It's about being codependent with the ones that I cherish. The way that my mother showed that she cherished me was to be codependent with me. That's how I was loved and that's how I learned to love. Seeing it for what it is has set me free. Envisioning the long lineage from mother to daughter to mother to daughter set me free. It's not that I won't stop being codependent. I could see that I would always have codependent tendencies connected with love, but then it would no longer be able to wound me and confuse me the way that it has in the past. I could see the topography of codependence laid over my heart but I could see that there were other lines, other tones that were innocent, pure, unconditional and courageous. My codependence was now part of a harmonic chord that was beautiful. Lifetimes went into the making of the way I love. I was so validated and excited about this realization that I could not get back to sleep.

I AM THE SEAM

Yesterday I had a very deep and difficult catharsis. I was embracing the aspect of me that feels rejected by humanity. It was extremely painful all the way into my bone marrow, my spinal cord, my immune system, my entire physiology was involved. I knew it was right because when I got close to embracing all of it I felt that I was deep in the crease of the catchers mitt, the seam where opposites meet. I could feel that quality of singularity, of collapsing all dualities. I wondered then if I was the seam. It made so much sense that the most intense feeling of lack and abandonment would line up with abundance and belonging. In order to experience the infiniteness of ourselves we need to have a deep and personal and direct experience of the opposite, the limitations of being on this earth. No more hiding and pretending and soldiering on. Feel the depths of anguish and the bewilderment of why it is so hard to be real. Not to indulge in these feelings but to bring them into the light. Our job is to live this life, feel the agony of not being seen, of being abandoned, betrayed, rejected and kicked out of the club. Our job is to bring our awareness into the darkness of humanity. You don't have to fix it or resolve it, you just have to be there. That's all. You're welcome to experience the infinity of all that is but if you want to experience being the seam, you have to greet the densest layer with your body. You have to feel it.

If your body is the multidimensional portal, that's the only way for you to take complete ownership of your portal. I own my portal. My body is, was and always has been the portal for every experience that I have ever experienced in this life and all my past lives as well. This is the practice of eradicating the programming from our portal so that we can take ownership. The way to eradicate the programming is to embrace it and embrace it all. This is my truth and this is part of me claiming it and owning it as mine. I own my portal! Now I understand the resonance that I feel when another takes ownership of their portal. What comes through them is pure creation. Inspired wisdom. This is how we create reality.

I am standing in the sun doing my practice asking why it took me so long, why at the ripe age of 64 do I have this realization? I am hit with the understanding of the neural connections, the inter-linking web of neural connections in my brain that was necessary to be in this position right here and right now. Then the sense of what an absolute privilege and honor it is to be here washes over me. I see and feel the symmetry of my experience; greeting the effect that rejection has had on my body, this utter devastation to my nervous system and its opposite, the complete and absolute assurance of the privilege and the honor of being alive in this moment.

I KNOW WHAT THE SINGULARITY IS

I know what the singularity is. Or at least a part of it I am glimpsing today. It's when enough of us recognize that we are but pieces on the chessboard. When enough of us realize that we are pawns, then the Chessmaster has lost control over us. I'm not saying this right, this is not quite it. It's more profound and simple than that. Those of us who think they are in control will also be freed from being in control, that's the singularity because no one really is in control. It's all a story, it's all a movie, a picture, a painting, a representation of life that is real in the way that a movie is real but it has no life outside of your attention. It's not as real as you are, and I am, it's not as real as the I AM of it all. What I had this morning, while sipping my coffee, was a vision of those that we think are in control becoming completely transparent. That is what's happening, that's what's being titrated into our collective identity, drop by drop. The balance of power, which was inverted, is righting itself. Can you feel it? You have to step out of the movie. You have to step off the timeline in order to really see it. So the singularity is that wave of realization that it's all a movie. The sensation in your body is an *aha!* experience; *oh! this isn't real!* So the singularity is a wave of realization. It's enough people realizing, sensing in the body in real time, that this is all a movie. It's not a thought, not a concept, but a feeling, a sensation in one's core that this reality is not all there is.

If the body is the portal then we would have to feel the new world. We would have to show up in the new world, physically.

Imagine what would happen to your nervous system if all of the locks of belief were taken off? What would your spine feel like? What would your body feel like? What would your heart feel like? You cannot control this wave. It's unstoppable.

Here's another way of seeing it. There are all these self-help programs that say about manifestation; envision having what you want, imagine it, align your energy with it and it shall come to pass. But everyone is saying I want to be the one who's controlling the pieces on the chessboard and what I'm saying is, no you don't! Because as long as you're working, trying to become the controller, as long as you're trying to be the one who moves the pieces, you're still stuck in the game of 3D reality, you're still stuck in the movie.

Now, as long as you draw breath as a human, you will be in the story. You will be in the movie. The movie won't end. But there's so much more to you! There's more to you than this movie. The larger part of you lies below it and beyond it. Most of you lies hidden below the tip of the iceberg, below what you can see and what's below is melting. The world doesn't end when the way it looks is washed away. The world grows into something that some of us are just beginning to glimpse. Reality is melting into the sea of consciousness.

Melting icebergs are feeding the phytoplankton and the plankton are feeding the krill and the krill are feeding the whales. Here's an interesting fact I just learned, whales feed on krill. Once a whale's belly is full and they have digested their meal they come up to the surface and they take a massive dump. The load is full of nutrients that feed the phytoplankton! It's a cycle! The phytoplankton are also feeding the coral reefs. Everything is getting nourished. Everything is being given the life that was once frozen below. What happens in the macrocosm is reflected in the microcosm. It's happening right now. If you have eyes to see you can see it. The singularity is happening right now. If it weren't happening, I couldn't see it.

I'm not saying that you are not creating this reality because you are. The life in you, the life force in you is creating this reality. So, if you want to move those chess pieces around, become a force of nature, become one with an unstoppable wave and the pieces will move in the direction that you are moving. You won't be controlling anyone else and no one will be controlling you. That's the singularity, the magnificent and magical reality. Each one of us rides our own wave. It is grace.

GLIMPSING IMMORALITY

I am having this recurring experience, almost always in the morning. I do this big stretch and when I draw back inward, I feel an indescribable sensation. I'll try to describe it. I sense myself as a giant, galactic encyclopedia of knowledge, wisdom, whimsy and love. Sometimes it's so overwhelming that I just burst into tears. The sensation is so exquisite. Perhaps I am glimpsing immortality. Perhaps when people transition this is how it looks and feels. When I let go of my resistance I can cross over. And cross back. No wonder my mind is freaking out. My mind says, *"this is not real!"* Or is it? So I'm asking the larger part of me, beyond my mind, what is this?

My mind is trying to identify and categorize the shift in my nervous system. But it can't. My nervous system is shifting out of linear time into timelessness. The new reality, fourth and fifth dimensional reality doesn't actually work in a way my mind can understand. So my mind can never fully understand what's happening because my mind only works in retrospect. Unless somehow there is a multi- dimensional mind? Or perhaps I am giving birth to a new identity and a new way of mind. Now mind. Timeless mind. Free mind. Never mind.

CONNECTION

Longing for connection is finally taking me down to seeing the connection even with those that don't want to connect with me fully or deeply or in any way, but there's still a connection. And the connection is actually quite deep. I see the connection even if they don't. I feel the connection even if they don't. It makes me feel alone, but in the loneliness, there's the absolute assurance, the reality that I'm not alone. It's a very odd, paradoxical feeling. But the fantasy escape hatch, where I am awash in the illusion that this person is connecting with me, with my heart, that they see me and want me, I'm seeing it for what it is. It's losing its hold on me. It's good because love becomes a choice and not a need. There's the hope of these moments of connection; when someone on some level actually gets where I'm coming from, responds in kind, and immediately forgets that they did, yeah, sad, but it's a nod from the universe. They are connected with me. That touches my heart. And sadness is gonna take me where I need to go. Home.

LONGING CONNECTS YOU WITH CONNECTION

Longing connects you with everything.

Spend Christmas alone. Let the sadness of the end of childhood dreams be your only companion on this day. Let the hollow well of longing take you. Let yourself drown.

On Christmas day a giant beneficent guide, bigger than anything I had known before, picked me up and presented me with gifts of awareness and gifts of insight. I was compelled to not make plans for the holidays, to stay in and be quiet. So that Santa could come. So that I could let go of the static and the memory of loss of family which I still grieve. The superficiality of the Christmas spirit is such bullshit. Few are satisfied. Most are compromising, getting a little tiny bit of what they really want. Mostly they've given up. Most adults have given up on magic. If you continue to feel the longing for magic, the intensity becomes unbearable. Recently, that intense longing awakened in me and I just let it have me. I let it take me until I finally got to this place where longing is connected to connection. Longing is connected to everything that I really want. There's no other way than to drown, to be pulled to the depths, to be pulled into desperation and loneliness and embrace it until you discover it can't kill you. You discover the sweetness of pure longing. What dies are all the strategies, all the trying, all the working and hoping to improve yourself so that you can be a better place to receive your heart's desire. That's my Christmas gift to myself and the world.

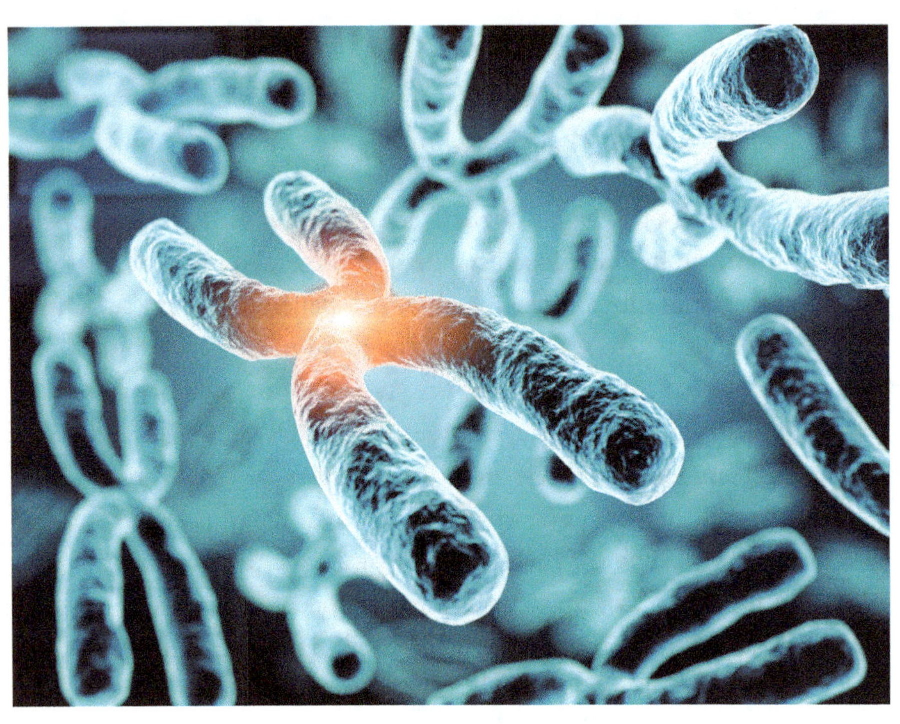

While I wasn't sleeping last night I was imagining talking to some friends about being a pawn on the chessboard. When you fully embrace that you are a pawn, you get to be the whole chessboard as well. Once you are the chessboard, then you can drop through the chessboard into more of who you really are. While I was imagining saying this, I again felt the chronic pain in my low back. I must have fully embraced being a pawn of my pain because suddenly, I was dropping through the chessboard. I was dropping through the chess game of my pain. My body began to writhe and rock energetically. My whole body was convulsing in a kind of ecstatic spasm. Then I saw the brightly lit X's of my chromosome pair. In my vision, my body was doing the DNA dance. My low-back was the pulsing center of the X. My upper body and arms were the top half of the X and my legs were the lower half. The very center of my body was the center of the X of my genetic code. I was seeing my genetic code shifting. I was releasing weak bonds, releasing weakness that was written into my genetic code. There's a reason what I saw was the X; female coding, female wiring, programming about being female such as being less-than and being a beast of burden because I am a woman. It's not just women who have this programming. Men have their own version of being a beast of burden. I was seeing how deeply it's tied to my identity. At one's core, deep within the center of the X, you carry the world on your back. I was seeing and feeling my body shedding this program. It's time to drop the world and be free.

I'm wondering if I've distilled my longing for companionship, connection and resonance into its purest form, which isn't form at all. It's more like a current of longing. It's the longing channel. When I'm in this channel, I feel the embodiment of the sacred in my humanity. And it's glorious. Imagination is striking out on its own. I see my sacred anatomy. I see and feel colors and patterns coming from different parts of my body, the liquid of my eyes, the ether of my throat.

The part of me that yearns for connection is connected. It's not about me. I don't have to draw a conclusion about my shortcomings based on my longing. This is new. I don't have to try and solve the problem by arranging get-togethers or going on a dating site. I don't have to wonder what it is I'm doing or not doing that puts me in this position of longing. The more that I open the floodgates to this pure longing, the stronger it gets and the less it becomes about me. I am being pushed around by it. I'm being carried by it. There's so much life force in it that I can't resist it. What if I stop seeing it as a hole in my life and start seeing it as an opening to other worlds? What if my heart's desire is riding on the current? All I have to do is keep jumping in. I'm being shown that it is one of the sweetest and purest of emotions. It's the launching pad for Esther Hicks' "rockets of desire." It makes the world move. It's not money that makes the world go round. It's longing.

THERE IS NOWHERE THAT I AM NOT

I imagined saying this to my daughter last night and when I did, everything shifted. I have often seen myself as the universe that my daughter dwells in, but it suddenly hit me that my mother or the Great Mother is the universe that I dwell in. There isn't any place that she isn't. The support that I need is everywhere. Instead of not feeling supported by anyone, everyone is here to support me. My kiss goes out to the universe and there is nowhere that is not kissed. As the great mother longs for my return, this is my longing. On Christmas day I went home or I should say I was home. Because I didn't go anywhere, but home came to me. Home came through me.

MICAHS DREAM LAST NIGHT

January 28, 2023

I was up above Ledbetter Beach on a sunny day in Shoreline Park. I heard the sound of a young man's voice, very happily singing nearby. Eventually I saw him. He was in an ornately colorful tee shirt and bright running shoes, running up the trail, singing at the top of his lungs. He ran right by me and I said, "I love your singing."

He smiled sweetly and kept on singing as he ran by. Then it hit me, that was me, 44 years ago, running on the trails on the cliffs above Surfer's Point at UCSB. I was one of a kind, a singular woman running free in 1979. At that time there was a growing wave of female athletes and I was riding the crest of that wave, running the trails above the ocean and dancing alone in the magic of that place. I was a trailblazer for an exponentially growing number of others who were now, many years later, moving and playing in joyous and unconventional ways. That I was having a realization during a dream is very odd, very different, and beautiful. Because I was in the dreamscape, it really opened up, and suddenly the whole of Shoreline Park was covered in what looked like white shaving cream. I could walk through it. A tunnel formed around me as I walked through the foam. At this point, I found my little brother Mitch, who is very much alive and my Mom and Dad, who are both deceased. I gathered them up and led them through these foam tunnels, walking across shoreline park. We were all holding each other's hand for reassurance while the tunnels formed around us as we walked. Then the foam cleared. It turned into a fog and just melted into the air. Now I could see across the park at Shoreline drive, the road that runs parallel to the park and cliffs and ocean below. There were two men in starship uniforms walking on either side of the road, although they might have actually been benevolent aliens. Whoever they were, they were part of the liberating army, the celestial Army Corps of Engineers and they were marching our liberation down shoreline drive. I heard, *"It is done. They are finally here. We are free."*

I started to cry. The officers were levitating between them, as they walked down the road, a floating, giant arch that went 50 feet up into the air. It was made of interconnected silvery metal Jax that looked like the metal Jax in the game from my childhood. It was magnetic. The function of the giant arch was to magnify the deep wisdom and guidance that was everywhere and it allowed you to be telepathic to hear and feel the guidance. It was also protection from the dissonant vibrations, the lies, the fear mongering, the old paradigm. But it was the kind of protection where all you had to do was pay attention and hear the wisdom and you were no longer enslaved. Now we were part of the galactic community, our star family, the new paradigm. Beneficent forces were here to nourish and protect us. Then, a short distance behind the arch there walked, in long loping strides, two giants! They were 18 feet tall or maybe even taller. One of the giants saw that I saw him and he took my free hand in his giant hand and shook it. He said, "We are here in the New Earth." Then we walked over to the cliff's edge to look down at Leadbetter beach. Extending across the sand was the same material the arch was made of. Lines of interconnected metal jax were laid across the sand and running down into the water. Then I began to see merpeople. They were swimming rapidly and powerfully with their great green fishtails. They seemed to be assisting with the implementation of these magnetic lines going down into the ocean. A merman jumped up out of the water, all the way to just below where I was standing on the cliff, grabbed something off of the edge of the cliff, and then dropped back into the ocean. I was laughing and crying, because we finally arrived in the world of pure magic. Then I woke up.

Later that day, when I was out and about in Santa Barbara, I looked up at those glorious green foothills, at the misty clouds surrounding them and everything looked different. I wondered if I had been given a glimpse of the other side of the veil. I wondered if those mythical creatures were already here. All of it was already happening and we just can't see it because we're in a different dimension.

SELF DRIVING BODY 2 - EFFORTLESSNESS

I've been having the experience of taking a few steps forward, it almost feels like falling because my usual locus of control is gone and something else has taken over my body. I have an experience of my body that is outside of my control. My body is in control of itself, driving itself without the "driver", which is my separate, conditioned identity. The self-driving body is being driven by a non-localized force. I probably have this all inverted. My experience is probably inverted. Or perhaps I'm finally having an experience of the inversion of this 3-D reality. I think that I'm having a momentary awareness of the mass insanity that we are the drivers of our body when actually we are not and never have been. This idea feels very close to the truth. Effortlessness is a quality of the self driving body. Effortlessness and paradoxically, control. This flies in the face of the definition of control but it is leading me into a sense of control that is so deep and so profound that it has nothing to do with power over anyone else, or power over myself even. It is Order. Cosmic order reveals itself when the body takes over. If enough of us can tap into this internal locus of control, of cosmic order, there will not no longer be a need for government. The inner locus of control just took a very, very deep sigh. I am knowing, feeling and sensing threads in the weave of a larger reality. How can a bird fly so effortlessly? Is it the same internal governor? I sense once again that I am being shown the keys to the Kingdom. I feel a deep spring of wisdom that is a sensation combined with information. Sensation that informs. Sensation that informs; releasing the body from what I think the body is, freeing myself from the stagnation of crippling programming. This Spring that wells up within me, it is the source of the reality that I am in the continuous process of creating.

Doing and being are one. Ultimately the fusion of one's conditioned identity with their larger self opens the door to their emancipation, the moving communion with pure presence. Ask the question: who is doing this movement? Who is moving this body? This grows your awareness of and perception that there is something grand behind, below and around who we think we are. During my practice I come into sacred communion with the source of my being.

COYOTE MEDICINE

Coyote is often seen as the trickster or the fool in the tarot deck. Coyote medicine is being willing to be the fool, to be seen as a fool, when, in truth, you're not participating in the status quo, you're not participating in the system. You are not caught up in the spells that others are casting and so you're actually free to be who you really are. You're in the world but you are not of the world. And you don't care, you don't mind how others perceive you or if they perceive you at all.

A coyote walked up to us, like it was nothing. It was the end of a long day of skiing at Mammoth Mountain. After the sun had set and we were about to leave the parking lot, a coyote trotted over the black and gray ice which was refreezing on the pavement, and just stood there, gazing at us. His coat matched the melting snow banks and the gray of the fading light. He seemed to say, *"You're in my world now. Welcome."* In the winter twilight, on the mountain road, it did feel very much like we had entered his world. We had stepped out of ordinary reality. All day I had noticed myself moving among people at the lodge, and on the ski slopes, they could see me, and I could see them, and yet I knew that I was in a completely different world than them. It was effortless and odd, yet exquisitely beautiful. I was simultaneously ordinary and extraordinary. It's because I let go of fitting in.

I seem to be in the midst of a shift in how I reference my body and, in that shift, how I reference my location in reality. It's still disorienting, It still makes me feel dizzy and slightly sick, but less than it used to be. I seem to be in the phase of titrating up a completely different locus of control of "who" is driving this body. My perception is that there is "me", who I think myself to be and then there's something surrounding me which is benevolent and self existent. A mighty companion in constant communion with me. I have also had the image of a key in a lock. It seems that my individual personality is the key, and the larger consciousness is the lock. I've gotten to this place as the key where I can actually fit into the keyhole of the lock. That's how it feels, and it is intensely gratifying. I dwell within this larger self, this larger consciousness but I'm actually experiencing it as a sensation. It's not a concept, it's not an idea, it's a sensation and has very much to do with how I experience myself moving through reality. It makes reality less fixed and more malleable, more uncertain, but also more of a thrill.

I can be in the state of malleable reality for a while, and then it b ecomes too much and I have to lie down. But I don't want to lie down. I want to go out and do things. I want to do things in a new way, in the malleable way. So I've been venturing out and failing, mostly, at being malleable. Mostly, I fall back into my default mode of trying to plod through. Or I give in to the fatigue, and I just lay down and take a nap. Drawing upon emotional energy may be my saving grace. The deep emotion that comes from source, almost like essence, springs up from deep inside. I have a slight headache. Feels like I have a bit of a cold. I want to transmute my cold. Trying to find the delicate balance between doing and being. Between surrendering to the heaviness and the achiness, embracing it and then saying now what? Now what? Not fighting it. Even though there's discomfort. Even though there's a sense of very deep fatigue. Not fighting it. Feeling it, and saying what else is there?

Self-awareness - this magnified self awareness is trying to happen every day. It can only happen if I'm in a place where no one else is around me. I'm just notating this again because I need to keep reminding myself that it's OK. It's OK to be alone. My heart is as big as the moon. Perhaps my longing for connection and communion is as big as the moon, I don't know. There may be a way that I can offer connection at some point instead of waiting for it to be offered to me. This may be why I keep seeing myself as the moon.

Each movement during my practice is showing me the sovereignty of the energetic that is me. The profane becomes sacred. Just standing here, moving my feet from a shaded area into the warmth of the sun, even that becomes sacred, showing me that what I thought was insignificant is actually extra- important. It's like going before a master and bathing in her gaze of complete unconditional love and acceptance but instead of the master guru, it is my own self-awareness that is seeing me with this pure light.

This has something to do with changing my beliefs about space. Being in space, but space is not separate from me. I could say I am in space but it's more like I am creating the space around me all the time. I think that's at the root of my perception earlier about the mundane being sacred. Because everyday space is considered mundane, profane. It's not sacred. They even have the name "sacred space" for temples and churches and power spots in nature. But if you're continuously in the process of creating space then all space is sacred.

I AM BONES

I am bones

I am grass

I am moans

I am groans

I am the sound of creation

There is nothing

Nothing

Nothing

Between me and me.

STAND NAKED

Bring yourself fully into the present moment. Stand naked, drop all of your personas, drop your emblems of power, drop your false humility, stand in the uncertainty, the anguish, the longing, the achiness, the weakness, the heaviness, whatever it is, just stand naked in it for a moment, show it to yourself and let it show through you. In this way, by sensing and feeling into all of these qualities that you cover and hide and shun, you gradually sense the composition of it, you sense what your pain is made of. When you sense what your pain is made of you realize you made it. Because you make everything out of what you are made of. When you sense the pain is made of you, you fall in love with yourself, even for the pain you made. Because it's all the same. Then you sense that there is no difference between the difficulty and the pleasure. It's just a different quality of energy. When you get here you can summon whatever quality you like because you're down to sensing what it's made of. Now you truly are in choice. But you have to get naked first.

It's an error of the mind to think that any spiritual system can take you where you need to go. But go ahead and engage and commit to whatever yoga, meditation, new age or healing modality that inspires you and fills you with purpose and motivation. Go ahead and build that bridge to nowhere. And when you find yourself on the edge of the cliff, having used up all the resources and materials at your disposal, and you're looking out at a vast and open emptiness, know that you have finally arrived. Now you can start the real journey.

If you want to step through the veil, then know that you created that veil. The veil is made of the same thing you are made of. Everything is made of what you're made of.

IS YOUR MIND A GOOD SERVANT TO YOU?

AIs your mind a good servant to you or are you a servant to your mind? Are you a slave to your mind? Do you do your mind's bidding? Who is the master?

Who or what is moving your body? What is this movement doing? What is this movement creating? Fully commit your movement to the unknown magic, the unknown mystery, the unknown realms that dwell within you and come through you.

Sonic boom: when the integrated movement reaches a singularity, and you suddenly find yourself in a new reality that you just created. You feel yourself as both the creator and the creation, and there may be a sound that wants to come through you. The sound marks the crossing of a barrier, a threshold, like the sonic boom, crossing the sound barrier. Gabriel's horn. The Call.

Taking action in the world becomes something very different now. Action becomes invention.

Beware the mind's mischief. Interpreting what you sense with what you already know is just slowing you down. How should I think about this? Whatever you think about it, don't take it seriously. There's so much more going on than what the mind can grasp. Say to your mind, *I am Sacred.* Then put your hands and heart to work shaping your own reality. No more maintaining an external reality.

DOUBLE BIND

Do you see the double bind of trying to change a world that is held together by what you believe?

How do you change your mind? How do you change beliefs? How do you break from your indoctrination? If you find yourself feeling like you've been put under a spell, you are on to something. Can you escape the collective spell that you've been put under?

When you see the programming for what it is, when you see the limitations laying upon your physicality, like heavy scales, like an armor you put around yourself, it's a bittersweet realization. When you discover that you've held yourself in this tiny form for so many years and so many lifetimes, all you can do is weep because you can feel the sweet edge of freedom, like a chilly breeze, like a chilly wind, lifting the scales, and brushing the tender, unformed skin beneath. The thing that keeps you in limitation is the same thing that can free you. It's a riddle, a koan that stops your mind and frees you from the double bind. Find yourself.

SWEET MEDICINE

You are the healing instrument. You are the magic wand.
You are the portal. You are the Stargate. You are the sacred
geometry. I read somewhere that the Indigenous tribes of the
Dakota plains where I grew up had an expression for the power
of nature. They called it Sweet Medicine. That has intrigued me
ever since I read it, because nature spoke to me and I listened.
I see the power all around me. I feel the medicine in Nature.
When I was a teenager I was so enthralled by nature I made
a leather belt with the words Mother Earth carved on it. The
earth is in constant communication with me, with all of us.
There's not a question that won't be answered by nature if you
stop and just pay attention.

Sweet Medicine comes right out of the air. Feels like medicine,
acts like medicine, smells like medicine, tastes like medicine.
Medicine that comes from beyond, gets picked up by the senses
and takes the form of whatever the body needs, whatever is
familiar in ordinary reality. Skip the step of identifying it as
vibrational or spiritual or transcendental. Skip the identification
all together. Just jump past the mind and be in direct experience. Later, after the experience, let the mind go to town trying
to digest what just happened.

DENSITY

There's a belief among spiritual seekers about the higher self, and about divine beings, that high vibration is good and low vibration is bad. What is sacred is of a high vibration and what is profane is low vibration. Often density is regarded as a low vibration and to be avoided or raised to a higher vibration.

Don't avoid density. It may not feel very good, but it is a necessary component to your beingness as a divine creation. It's built into you. You must face it. If you descend down into the nether regions of yourself, you will find the molecular structure, the atomic attraction, gravity, density. If you go deep enough into your density, you come out the other side. So density is a portal into your next creation. Density at its absolute compactness becomes a black hole. An opening which portals you into a blank slate, pure nothingness, an empty canvas where your new reality will be painted. In reality this is happening on an atomic scale. An endless circle of creation and destruction, although nothing is destroyed. It's just pulled into potential and pressed back out onto the fabric of creation. This is the pulse of life, the heartbeat, the breath. If you truly embrace who, and what you are, you come to an awareness of your density.

ZERO POINT

When I bring my energy back to the zero point I see everything and I know everything.

I'm shown everything I need to know in the moment regarding the conditions that are around me with a clarity and a reality that's more than a conceptual understanding. It's alive. It's a direct experience of truth.

Reality is enhanced by your presence, enhanced by you letting more of yourself appear. Everything looks brighter, and more vivid, because you are brighter and more vivid. Relax your beliefs that there is any authority outside of you, external to you. The mathematics and the geometry of reality may appear to sit outside of you, but is it? Or is reality far more mysterious and unfathomable than science could ever measure? Can you be the creator of reality and the creation? Are the levers of creation within your grasp or are they outside of it?

THERE'S A DARK RESIDUE

Mother's Day, 2023

There's a dark residue of Motherhood, a dark film that rests on the edge of everything that you view. It's been hidden, pushed down into the subconscious but now it's coming to light. It's a belief about where you lie in the hierarchy. The most precious thing that you have to give is found wanting. Your love is not enough. It's why you've tried to be so strong. To prove your worth. But your worth has nothing to do with the hierarchy. As you finally feel it, this layer of pain that's been hidden for so long, and it's finally being washed up to the surface, as you sit in this unbearable place where the most precious thing you have to give is not enough, as the grief overtakes you and your body weeps, you hear another voice. This voice is saying what a profound gift you're giving to the world at this moment, by letting the emotions run through you, by allowing this realization into your larger self, which goes beyond the hierarchy and goes beyond duality. The value of your existence can't be measured. It is beyond measure. You finally land in the true meaning of motherhood, in what it means to give birth, to allow creation to come through you. Give yourself time to feel what this is on this day, Mother's Day. Give yourself time to sit in this release, and the relief in the realization of your true nature. Let your body re-form. Let yourself take a new form that is softer and easier as the film, the residue continues to release out of your blood and bones and brain and nervous system. Feel how your body has been held captive by this invisible film. Feel how your form has been held in limitation and contraction in the battle of duality, and now you are free. You are no longer at war with this belief. Allow the absence of the dark line that used to inform you. Allow the milky whiteness to permeate every part of you. Allow yourself to not know who you are now and who you will be. Know this: any belief that you have about yourself is a limitation. It could very well be that you set yourself up to take on and then unwind these self-limiting beliefs. Come to the realization that you are more, much more than you ever thought, or believed that you could be. You did it on purpose as a gift, both to yourself, and to the world. Those are thoughts, but the feeling is just to sit here and be radiant, be a radiating milky whiteness of pure potential.

Feel yourself moving without the motivations that are now gone. You may not want to move at all. You may just want to sit still and notice the world coming toward you. A new, unfamiliar world. Or perhaps you're feeling a part of yourself that you're unfamiliar with. Be gentle. Go slow. Find your way.

SELF LOATHING

I was standing in my parking lot this morning when a possum walked up to me and just sat there for quite a while, looking up at me. I'm wondering if the possum has a message for me about a feeling I had been struggling with all day yesterday: self loathing. Playing possum. Play dead. Because self-loathing is a kind of death. It shuts me down. And yet this morning when I'm looking at it, I'm seeing that it can't be avoided. It can't be helped. There's a thread of self loathing that's a part of me. It will always be a part of me and I need to accept it. I need to embrace it. I need to stand naked in my self loathing and say *so be it*. When I do this I find there's a delicateness and a sweetness inside of my self-loathing. Possum medicine?

YOU ARE BEGINNING TO RECOGNIZE YOURSELF

You're catching glimpses of yourself creating your reality. This is the real you. So many happy tears. The other qualities of you in your 3D life are real too, but they are copies. They are paintings drying on the canvas, whereas when you glimpse the real you, you glimpse that you are the painter and the paint. It's more than that. It's a glimpse of how the world emerges through you. It's a glimpse of how the world is because of you, because of how you are. The world changes depending on how you are. That's what you're starting to see. Not an idea, not a concept, but more of a shape. The shape of the world is sculpted by the shape that you are in. And you are not a constant. You are not fixed. You are in a constant state of change, of flux, of movement, of pulse, of breath. Nothing stays the same. You cannot hold onto who you were a millisecond ago. You can hold onto the memory of it but it's only a memory. It's a copy. It's not who you are anymore.

This is hard. This makes me uneasy and it makes my stomach churn. Or maybe it's my stomach that's churning out this information. My stomach is digesting an experience that my body has never had before. All day long the songs on the radio have been sacred chanting from different religions and different disciplines. Right now it's a Latin liturgy being sung with such devotion. It's almost as if the universe is rising up to greet me. My crystal is telling me I can travel without going anywhere. I'm holding it right now and seeing myself in a sort of a spiritual emergency room. There's a bunch of us here. It's also like taking a class. It's like a class of energy Masters. It's all a part of this transformation, so it's expected that people might feel a little sick or a little weak and not be able to move. It's an expected part of the class.

WORDS FROM THE BODY

As you extract yourself from right or wrong, good or bad, pleasure or pain, strength or weakness, as you extract yourself from duality, the words are more simple and basic. They are the sounds of nature, not the intellect, not the library of concepts. Words from the body rise up as sensations that inform the mind and the words don't make any sense in the relative perspective of conditioned reality. Words from the body rise up like waves with a sound and a feeling that is unmistakably natural. It's spring, and you are beginning to bud and bloom.

Move and ask nothing of the body, except what the body wants to tell you with its movement. Not in words, but in sensation, perhaps images, perhaps sounds. When you stop and listen, not just with your ears but with your heart, listen with your emotions. Drop down below everything you know. Drop down into the source of you. What do you see and feel here in this place? What arises from this place? And if you close your eyes, go inside and listen for a while and then you open your eyes and the world outside looks different, the light is different, the birds sound different, it is because the world comes through you. A new world appears. You are not the same.

Let your body sink down. Inhale. Sweep your arms down below you and scoop up the liquid light, the spring of source energy, scoop it up into your body, into your legs, into your hips, into your pelvis, into your torso up and into your organs and lungs, breathing source energy. Breathe source energy and let your body speak.

EMBRACING THE ONE WHO PLODS AND PLOTS

I am dancing in this part of me that needs to slow things down and analyze every move that I make. When I speak from this place, it's with a plodding, hesitant voice. It appears to me now as an outline of who I thought I was. I'm seeing how I've drawn myself into the world. I'm seeing that I am more than the drawing. It's an amazing feeling, to no longer be subject to but instead dancing with the one who plods and plots. It's a feeling of softness and poise and illumination and freedom. This is a part of me that is not gonna go away. I'm celebrating the plodding part of me.

I was out in the front doing my practice this morning and I was thinking about how I could get in touch with this person that I missed seeing yesterday. As I was thinking about it, these two crows flew right over my head and they were cawing and as they were cawing, they cawed right into my thought process. Those crows were coming into my thoughts, they were talking to me. They were saying the answers are all around you. You don't have to work it out inside your head, inside your sense of isolation because you are not inside your head. The crows were saying not even the one that plots and plods is separate from all that is. In that moment the part of me that felt so alone, and has worked so hard to make it safe for me in the world, became a part of something bigger. I'm having a sensation of such spaciousness and ease, it's really quite profound.

Today I was given an impression of the part of myself that plods and plots and conjures and thinks that it is in charge of me. I was given the impression that it isn't. I was given an impression that it was just a layer of the multi-layered being and presence that I am.

IF YOU KNEW HOW MUCH YOU ARE LOVED

If you knew how much you are loved you would weep with joy. As the depth and breadth of infinite love hits you, you will start to understand that you've always loved as much as you are loved. Then the drama around loving begins to untangle. There is no greater power in the universe than the love that comes through you, unfiltered, unabridged, untainted by heartbreak and betrayal. Pure love is with you, for you and of you.

You can, when you feel it, invite that infinite love into every place inside of you. And if you make this gesture toward yourself, you'll see, you'll discover that there isn't anywhere inside of you that love isn't. Love is inside all of your wounds too. Love is inside your pain and your conflicts, your dark thoughts, your depression, and your anger. Love is inside all of it.

NAUSEA

The nausea is from being non local. Like seasickness. Eventually you recover from the seasickness. And then you venture into another layer of non-locality, and you get seasick again.

SHOW YOURSELF TO YOURSELF

It's not so bad. The worst of you is connected to the best of you. And it's all being mixed together.

There is no distance between your victories and your mistakes. There is no reason to figure out what you did wrong because what you did wrong and what you did right are so intrinsically connected that it is impossible to separate them. There's no reason to sort yourself out. Ever.

Finding your frequency is bringing together all the differentiated aspects of yourself until there isn't one that you prefer or revere over another, so that it all becomes blended into one fine misty foam. And then you begin to find resonance with the truth, with the frequency, with the pure, fine essence of you. It's a familiar sensation. You'll recognize it when you feel it; a feeling that is so subtle and so deep within you and yet it is you. On some level it is being shown. On some level it is being seen. All the portrayal, the personas, the carefully crafted self images, they are nothing in the face of your frequency. The pure essence of your being is seen. It has always been seen. And what everyone is seeing is the very thing that you've always wanted to be seen. So you can relax. You don't have to sort yourself out for anyone. You don't have to explain yourself to anyone.

Frequency is a movement; it's not static, so it's never the same. Yet it is. The only way to grasp this frequency is to be in the form of a human being. This is a great achievement. This is mastery.

Here is the new social currency. It doesn't really matter what you think, it doesn't matter what you believe, the only thing that matters is the frequency, the pure essence that shines through you, and the more that you witness your own essence, the more your thoughts and beliefs come to reflect that. The more you say, "I am that," you tear open the world and step into a new way of being human. The new social currency is happening now. If you have eyes to see and ears to hear.

THE GIFT OF SELF LOATHING

Those of us who have felt such intense emotional pain, have the opportunity to access the depths of power that lie alongside that pain. This made me think of you, my friend, and how intense the pain is that you feel and I was thinking about some of my other friends, who sort of skip along on top of the ocean of emotion. Something happens when you go deep, something happens to you that gives you a precious gift. You are able to experience the depth of emotion. It makes you rare in the world and that brings up more emotion, because one who is able to feel so much also feels the loneliness of not being met by others who also feel deeply. We are a rare few.

I've been seeing a new way of social currency, where I don't have to be lonely anymore because all of the old beliefs that lie on top of how we interact are now seen for what they are. They're seen as a scaffolding that lays on top of something that's much more subtle and pure. If we can get down to the pure frequency of who you really are and who another person really is then we can let go of the obfuscation and the uncertainty and the trying to be a good person and all that bullshit and just be real with each other. This is a new way of being real.

Sometimes, in these moments of realization, I feel so powerful, and I feel like this is why I came. What I mean to do is to invite people into the pure frequency of who they really are. The only way that I can do it authentically is to be the pure essence of who I am. I've seen that as a huge challenge for years and years and now I'm seeing the end. I'm seeing a light at the end of the tunnel.

If you would just bring the part of yourself that you loathe into your heart, instead of running in the opposite direction, getting busy to make yourself feel better about yourself, if you would just bring that part of yourself into your heart, you would weep because you finally came home to yourself. This is all that this loathsome part wants, is to be welcomed home. When you finally welcome this part of you home, no matter how big it is, no matter how long it takes; when you finally stop running from it, and stop trying to prove yourself and stop trying to disprove all of the beliefs that underlie that self-loathing; that you were unworthy or that you're insignificant, unimportant, nothing that you do matters, you can't win, no matter what you do; whatever the source of the self-loathing, if you're someone like me, who's had years to foster and fester all of the poison juices, when you finally begin welcoming this part of you home into your heart, you realize that the compassion you feel is so profound and so huge that nothing can stop it, ever. Then you realize that you've given yourself a great gift because now you have the capacity of compassion that is a perfect match. You don't have to pretend that the poison isn't real. You don't have to pretend that it doesn't exist because you have the antidote. You have the pure essence of you which lies somewhere in between the poison and the potion. You have to go through the duality until you get to the essence of you which lies beyond duality, which has no attribute. Then you can only sit in awe of what you've discovered, and what you've discovered is your true nature has no attribute. It's not good or bad, it's not gentle and kind or rough and wicked. Just sit in the beautiful majesty of your own location, your non-local location which you can now feel. It is a feeling that runs through your body up into your chest, a feeling of belonging to yourself, and nothing else.

I AM MAKING A PACT WITH MYSELF

I am making a pact with myself

To keep creating blossoms.

My heart goes beyond my mind.

Quiet wisdom overrides reason,

Surrounds and embraces knowledge,

Shows me what lies beyond.

Fleeting perfection.

My innate takes over

As my personality waits and watches.

POWER SPOTS MAGNIFY WHAT WE KNOW

Power spots magnify what we know about
ourselves. About energy, about the illusion of
space and time. The true nature of our nature
is made visible and more accessible in power
spots. It washes over you.

Stand in the center of the bull's-eye. You are
the arrow that sprouts blossoms. As you tap
into the golden well, and the nectar shoots up
your spine, it illuminates your true nature.

IT DOESN'T MATTER

It doesn't matter what you used to separate from
yourself. The way back is the way in. It's so much
simpler than you think, now that you know why
and you can see the steps plainly beneath your feet.

You've traveled a long, long way to get back to
where you started.

I'm not a ghost.
I'm not an apparition.
I'm not what I think.

THE ERA OF DISRUPTION

I watched a TV show called Minx where nude males posed for magazine centerfolds in the 70s. The magazine became famous overnight because of the resistance to it. There were so many people against it that everybody wanted to know what all the fuss was about. So the magazine sold out within hours. It hit me that what's been going on since long before the 60's and 70s and now reaching a violent crescendo, is disruption. It doesn't matter what side you're on, it's the ones that are creating the biggest disruption that are getting the most attention. And it doesn't matter how absurd and ludicrous these people or their actions are, such as the biological male swimmer who is now the national champion of women's swimming. Or preceding that, the 2016 U.S. presidential election and the resulting conflagration in Washington with all branches of government exposing their dark underside. The absurdity is so obvious. We have asked for this disruption, we can't look away from this, we crave this, even though we think that we don't. Even though we think we want life to make sense, be smooth and stable and predictable. We have finally come to the level of consciousness, as a species, to see, en masse, how absurd our reality really is.

PAIN IS POWER

I went into pain, my sinus pain. I did the leaning back exercise, acknowledged the emotion that arose and leaned back some more. I leaned back into the source of my pain. At its source, pain is power. I had an experience of my own power, the power cord, the channel of power that's pure potential. It started as a tiny thin line of energy in the middle of my head, and then expanded down to show me that my core is pure potential. My core is power without attribute, which is just pure potential. I had never experienced power this way before; a taste of freedom. It's the freedom to be or do anything because I am the power source. And pain, if I don't fear it, if I don't try to solve it, is a doorway, an opening, a crack where the orange blaze of my power is shining through.

PLAYING DEATH LIKE AN ACCORDIAN

A colorful image of myself emerges as the Jester, as the wildcard, as the conjurer summoning the boundary of what's real and what's beyond reality. The trickster totem, the coyote, appears at the edge of my vision. I am no longer so afraid that I need to turn away from it. Instead, the rising buzz of dizziness forms like a swarm of electric bees between my hands. I am standing on the carnival stage playing it, the squeezebox made of death. My hands expand and contract while the buzzing swirls between them. I wonder if my role in life is naming things that can't be named, just for the fun of it. The question emerges about crossing over but it's not crossing over. It's being the dart in the epicenter of the rippling dartboard where the circles go on and on and on forever. Who can stand here? The Jester, the trickster, the coyote, the conjurer. I'm sure that's just a prelude to who or what is here. What is here is not a what but a how. What is here is the absence of a who. Jester is the only image that can be summoned that comes close. Because a jester is a costume with nobody inside of it. The joker can be any card in the deck. Let go of all your attributes and achievements. There's nothing left to do except be sung by your cells and be swung in the wind at the center of stillness.

I so love this place where I've never been before, in this spooky Carnival attraction, the House of Horrors. The whole place, now I get it, this whole town, this whole world is just one big creepy hall of mirrors. You have to be insane to believe that this reality is all there is. Perhaps your insanity can be cured.

SCRAPING THE BOTTOM OF THE BEAKER

Scraping the bottom of the beaker
for relevance.

The residue is all you see,
invisible alchemist,
Invisible even to yourself,
while the distillate,
The life that you are
rises up like a mist
And colors the world.

The Genie is out of the bottle.
Pandora has left her box
And she's showing you
what's left of your identity.

THE UNIVERSE BREATHES THROUGH US

The universe breathes through us
And shapes us
In its image.
All that is breathes through us.

Unlock the breath,
        Let it rumble.
                Let it roll.
Till the creaky wagon
That you thought you were
Starts to fall apart.
        Till the wheels fall off
                And away you fly.

And the lineage you leave behind,
Still dressed their 20th century finery,
Along the roadside stand in a tailored line,
All waving goodbye.
        As you sail out of sight.
                Laugh, don't cry.

Unlocking the breath
Invites the universe.
Breathe with me,
And I will show you
        Everything inside of me.
                The world within me.

HIGH TIDE

I am underwater.

Do you know the feeling?

Like trying to run in a dream.

I hear the mermaids singing,

"Stop struggling and breathe

      in the thick mixture.

You are the mixer.

You are the blender.

The sea is inside you."

HERE I AM

Languaging the ineffable.
Pulling up God's Rolodex;
Who shall we hear from next?
Galactic family taking turns in a sing-along?
Or a barefoot wanderer
Out on the fringe of the frontier
Where there is no address?
We hear you!
We know you're out there!
Out there is in here where I am.

THINGS THAT MAKE THEMSELVES HAPPEN

Now you are the petal
Unfurling yourself just like
Wounds that heal themselves.
A line of power in your skin
Is all that remains.
Reminding you from whence you came.
Blooms and wounds are so close.
One is opening a closing
And one is closing an opening.

SUMMON YOURSELF

Summon yourself.

    Summon all of you home

        inside.

Assemble yourself.

    Assemble your temple.

Ride the inspiration.

    Rise into the steeple.

Open the bell tower and

    feel yourself ringing out

        across the cosmos.

Unstoppable.

There need not be a reckoning with all of your insides, with all the hard shapes and shadows that you've been running from. Your insides are holy land you didn't know was there. Return to the temple inside. You thought your body was a waste land. You thought your feelings were a symptom of your unease with living. Now I understand.

Assemble yourself.
Assemble your temple.

FORM APPEARING

I'm finally getting it, what's happening with my body. With all of our bodies. Our form appears in the present time. If you pay attention to the subtle sensation you can feel it. Imagine the Star Trek series, beaming out of one place and into another. Our bodies are not these fixed blobs of flesh stuck on a linear timeline. Here's another inverted reality revelation; how our bodies appear is not how it appears. It's reversed. We appear in form because we can. We beam ourselves into our reality. Your mind is so hungry to understand this but you can't, you have to feel it happen and as you feel it your mind goes, *what was that?* Because there's no frame of reference in our day to day reality to explain it. But science is catching on.

When I have the sensation of my form appearing in the present time, I feel like I am showing up in a potentially new timeline, or circumstance where beings who are not limited by the physical are there with me. I feel seen by a larger presence that I am inside of. This presence is seeing more of me than I usually see in myself; the sweetness of who I really am. All of my discomfort fades. The deep anxiety fades.

I was telling a friend about this experience of appearing in form or form appearing, and it occurred to me that the great level of anxiety and discomfort that many of us have been experiencing is due to our nervous system transitioning into a more subtle nervous system that can actually sense and feel as we appear in form. Once we get used to our new, improved nervous system we experience the opposite. We feel better than we have in a while. We reach a completion of sorts, a resolution of our nervous system achieving its next level of functionality. The nervous system is now functioning beyond what is known in 3-D.

There are no special circumstances to appear in form. I heard this, as I was preparing to do my practice today, feeling a bit weary and worn out, doubting that I would be able to be present. This voice was saying that the special circumstances are created by my mind after I appear in form. My mind says well, it must be because I was in a great mood or I was well rested that I was able to fully be present to appearing in form. But this voice today said there are so many different threads and different ways that you can appear in form. It's not just one way, it's not what the mind is telling you.

LET YOUR DISCOMFORT CATCH UP WITH YOU

At the beginning of the day before you've worn yourself out running away from it, let your discomfort catch up with you. Let it wrap itself around you like electric chain mail, all the sharp edges making themselves known. Let yourself feel it until you hear its message, which may surprise you as you feel how precious you are. Dance with discomfort now.

I danced with my discomfort or maybe I should say, my discomfort danced with me and transmuted into something like energy or life force. I was shown that discomfort is not a threat. There are no threats. That's just a state of mind. A general state of unanswerable prayers. A state of feeling like you're falling when there's nothing to crash into but emptiness. Sing out the sound of discomfort and feel it mesh and merge into the fabric of your reality. This is a new way to start my day or to center my day and open the door to something new.

I look over at the kitchen table, my chair pulled out, my purse hanging over the back, my pen, notebook and phone on the table and my flip-flops on the floor, angled and ready to be donned. From where I stand, barefoot on my soft rug at the center of my living room, the woman who sits in that chair and writes in that notebook and scrolls through her phone is a different person than the one who stands here. The one who stands here just had another transcendental experience. The one who stands here is standing at the center of everything and is able to see the traces and the tracks of this other Micah, the Micah that plans and plots and plods through her day.

I stand here at the center of all things, looking down at Micah's shoes, and wonder if I could be the one to put them on and go out into the day.

You're like a miner picking through the density until you find the jewels. The joules. The current. The currency. The most sophisticated algorithms and AI systems are but a crude imitation of what you can do with a single breath. Pay attention to your breath, and you'll start to see, you'll start to have an idea of all that you have access to. The universe is yours.

THE PRICE YOU PAY

The price you pay
For bravely pushing yourself
Through imagined obstacles,
For scaling walls that you built,
For slaying monsters that you created,
For serving those you chose to love,
The price is your life.

Have you lived?

The gig is up.
I'm not paying anymore.
I'd rather collect coincidences
Like fireflies in a jar
And let them light my way.

I'd rather lean back on my couch
Of colorful, cosmic glow-worms
And let them spell out,
On the skin of my back,
In a new language made of sensation,
The truth of my existence.

THE WATERFALL

I made myself an offering

And into the pool I crawled,

On my hands and knees,

Naked in the shallow water,

Under the frozen gazes

Of the ancient's stone faces,

Till I reached the waterfall

And knelt on a rock altar

Made from the falling water.

My body was the offering

Crossing over without dying.

Then I felt her blessings,

In an endless cascade

That landed on me like kisses.

It was the end of me

And yet I'm still standing.

I AM A COMMON WOMAN

I am a common woman. I speak the common tongue, by choice, because the architect of worlds dwells within me. She speaks to me, in felt images, the secrets of the universe. But they are only secrets from the mind. The body knows. And the body is common to all. The architect of worlds dwells within all of us.

I am the translator of light language, in words that are felt before they are understood. Words that open parts of you that you didn't know you had. I cast spells to liberate you from the lexicon that has kept you in bondage. I am righting the inverted reality that you live in. By writing. In words that anyone can understand.

SITTING WITH STAR COMMAND

Sitting with Star Command,
Dumbfounded and slightly unwell
From being in two places at once.

They're not telling you the whole story.
They're not even speaking.
And yet they're showing you the way.
Feel their gaze upon you,
The steady green-gold gaze
That has seen the galaxy.

Let them show you the way.
It's nothing like you thought.
Not a bunch of separate units
Flying around
In shiny ships
And shiny space suits.
Let all that drop away.

It's more like a thick cream
Spread out over the stars
Connecting us.

The Milky Way
And you are the sweetener.

EMBRACE YOUR INSECURITY

Embrace your insecurity,
Until your insecurity
Embraces you.

Feel her caress your real shape.
Under the costume
You've forgotten how to remove,
You are a crimson rosebud.
There's nothing hiding in your folds
But softness
And the resting essence
Of gentleness
Waiting to open,
Waiting to show your velvet self.

Now you've done it.
There's no going back.
But why would you want to?
Where do you feel it most?
In your belly?
In your groin?
Can you feel the truth of it?
Can you feel the life in it?
Can you feel that this is the real you?
The emblem of your tenderness.
The anthem of your passion.
Without it, you can love,
But you cannot be in love

THE BASEMENT OF THE BASEMENT

If you ever reach

The basement of the basement,

    you'll find my initials

        carved on the door.

And some dried up petals

    from the rose I left you,

        wrinkled up on the floor.

You'll find the way back faster

And a little little bit smoother,

    from the footprints

        of those few who

Made the descent before.

MY BODY IS TAKING OVER AGAIN

I love this sensation of being folded and molded, and I heard the words, "it is as it always has been." I realize that this fluidity has always been going on. I just couldn't sense it because my identity was separate and outside of my body. This has always been going on but my perception was hijacked. That's how it feels now, like my perception was actually hijacked and was kidnapped and hidden in a room of mirrors where I could only see the aspect of myself that I was told I could see. This deeper, more fluid self, this generator, this shaper of reality is my true identity, and the odd thing is that it is devoid of personality. I guess my personality is here somewhere. I mean, I can feel a thread of it, but what I feel more is the absence of my personality obscuring what's really going on. I see the jagged edges. I see a broken shell with jagged edges but the teeth don't bite into me; they don't have any purchase. I no longer think that I am the illusion. I no longer think that I am the garment that I wear to move about in the Maya.

I wanna thank you again for reminding me just how precious, exquisite and beautiful I am. My heart is cracking open again. I'm being loved by the gods, acknowledged and treasured, I can feel the gates to my joy cracking open. I can hear the sound of ice beginning to break up and the sensation of a massive river of opportunity that's beginning to flow in my direction.

DO I DARE FEEL THIS GOOD

Sad self,

> "it won't last."

Expanded self,

> "that's right,

>> you can go back to

feeling shitty whenever you want."

THE WHALERS

Just below the equator

On an isle they call Moorea

There's a different kind of whaler

Chasing Humpback mamas and babies.

In a small boat filled with seekers

Armed with nothing but their bathers,

Who jump into the indigo waves

And swim against the breakers,

In hopes of coming face-to-face

With the oldest living ancients.

Just to make their acquaintance,

And glimpse and feel the greatness

Of the largest sentient creatures

To ever roam this place.

WHERE ARE YOU?

Most of the time you don't know where you are. Because what you know isn't where you are. So you can cling to the security of what you know and keep repeating the same old patterns and keep showing up in the same old places. But that's just a pinpoint, a period in the book, the volume of where you really are. Where you really are is standing in a field of potentials where just your attention sprouts new life up around your feet. It's not a concept. It's where your body really is. How do you get your awareness here? You honor all that you are, from the most subtle energetic to the densest aspect of your physicality. You honor all that has come before and all of the present time qualities and sensations within you and around you. When you do this you arrive at where you really are.

I SPEAK TREE

I speak tree

I speak with the breeze

So come over here

And give my branch a squeeze.

If your eyes

Start to wrap

    around the sides

        of your head

You start to see now

    instead

        of what's ahead.

You may catch a glimpse

Of your spooky Alien family.

They all speak tree.

LIFECYCLE OF A GRASSHOPPER

Some of us are coming out of the sticky phase.
Grasshoppers don't,
But who knows
If they dream, like me
Of becoming a butterfly?

This majestic green hopper
Laid claim to my roses.
Supposed to be lucky
So I let him stay.

It's nice to be out of the cocoon.
I have a body again.
Mostly out of pain.
Pain has changed
Into potential to bloom.

My new body is showing me
Realms within realms
Rising up at my feet.
Who needs wings?
Frailty becomes a thing
Multifaceted and sweet
As a honeycomb.
Inoculated by frailty.

Fearless grasshopper.
Lion on a leaf.
The camouflaged king
Of the Field.

DISSOLVING

Be ok with dissolving.

You can't reason with a dust devil.

You can't escape the swirl.

As you spiral down

Your feet find friendly ground.

Warm softness surrounds you.

Home in the land of openings.

Indestructible tenderness.

What was I afraid of?

INNOCENCE

My innocence is cracking open. The love that pours forth from this opening is washing away everything I knew about the world. Love is the truth, the only truth. Everything else is a fleeting roadside attraction. Something to say you saw on your journey. "Oh, isn't that interesting?"

I think, what a great achievement this is, to be in this realization, to get past all the bees protecting the hive and crack open the honeycomb, to get to taste my own honey. But, my innocence says, no, I don't know what this is. I don't know what I've done. I don't know what I've become. And this is where I want to be. In the space of not knowing, while a river of love carries me to I know not where.

COME OUT OF THE CAVE

Come out of the cave
Where you've been hiding.
Pull your darkness up from the depths
And shed your monster skin,
Over and over and over again.
Invoke the sacred pact
You made with the earth
A millennia ago.

The time has come.
The time to act.
Your magic light language is not exclusive
So share it with your neighbor,
With the grocer, the mailman.
Bring them all into your effervescent orb.

The Stargate grifters,
Priests and Priestesses,
Medicine men and Medicine women
Have no special knowledge
As they stand with their hands out
In front of their frozen icons.

You are the Stargate.
You are the Priestess.
You are the Medicine.
As you shed
what's dead
And remake yourself
over and over and over again.

SCRUFFY PERFECTION

When perfection becomes ordinary,

when perfection loses its edge,

what will you strive for then?

When there's nothing left

to compare yourself to?

When you look in the mirror

and see your scruffy perfection

looking back at you?

WE HAVE RETURNED

We have returned to repaint the pyramids
With alchemical gold.
We have returned to reignite
The fires of resurrection.
We have returned to restore the Temples
To their opulent glory.
We have returned to reopen the floodgates
Of the Sacred waters.
We have returned for the rebirthing
And reunion of our Star Family.
We are all
And all is One.

Micah Lee Malloy, LAc.LMT, is an athlete, shaman, and Zhineng Qi Gong Instructor. She developed a dynamic style of bodywork and movement that reaches into the subtle energetics of the physical form. After 40 years of practice in the field of alternative medicine, using only her body and senses as the instrument, she has concluded that the human body is in the midst of an evolutionary shift. A shift away from being a fixed, solid form and a fixed identity in a fixed reality. The whole point of an about me page is to give the reader some way to identify the author. But the author is wondering if she has a calling card that isn't confined to living on a two dimensional page. The author is asking you to ask this question as well. Meanwhile, if she is to be found it will be surfing the waves or hiking the foothills of the Santa Barbara coast, or refining her daily practice of Dimensional Movement.

IMAGE INDEX

Statue of Gabriel • Shutterstock 4

Blue on White Block Print • Sam Malloy 18

Dandelion Photo • Micah Lee Malloy 24

Mobile Kaleidoscope • Unsplash 32

"Air" (Eternal Vision) • Davia King 40

Micah's Logo (phi spiral)• Micah Lee Malloy 48

"Your Perspective"• Davia King 58

Crossing the Threshold • Micah Lee Malloy 66

Golden Concentric Triangles • Unsplash 74

"Heart Resonance" • Davia King 82

"Wonder" • Davia King 90

X Chromosome • Stock Image 98

Coyote • Micah Lee Malloy 106

Alive • Davia King 112

Tree With Pink Blossoms • Stock Image 116

Possum • Stock Image 122

Crow • Stock Image 126

"We are One" • Davia King 130

Neptune Roses • Micha Malloy 134

Jester Statue • Stock Image 140

"Water" • Davia King 144

"Holy Trinity" • Davia King 148

"The Portal" • Davia King 154

"Fire" (Full Potential) • Davia King` 158

Polynesian Whales • Daniel Kaiawe 164

Grasshopper • Stock Image 168

Micah at the feet of the Sphinx • Micah 174

Micah Lee Malloy • Rhonda Lee Johnson Photography........ 176